Gunilla Norris

Gunilla Norris

Sharing Silence

∙∙

Becoming Bread

∙∙

Journeying in Place

Quality Paperback Book Club
New York

Sharing Silence

Meditation Practice and Mindful Living

Contents

Foreword

Within each of us there is a silence
—a silence as vast as the universe.
We are afraid of it . . . and we long for it.

When we experience that silence, we remember
who we are; creatures of the stars, created
from the birth of galaxies, created
from the cooling of this planet, created
from dust and gas, created
from the elements, created
from time and space . . . created
from silence.

Silence is the source of all that exists,
the unfathomable stillness where vibration began
—the first oscillation, the first word,
from which life emerged. Silence is our deepest nature,
our home, our common ground, our peace.
Silence reveals. Silence heals.

Silence is where God dwells.
We yearn to be there. We yearn to share it.

And yet, in our present culture,
silence is something like an endangered species . . .
an endangered fundamental.
The experience of silence is now so rare
that we must guard it and treasure it.
This is especially true for shared silence.

Sharing silence with others is a political act.
Silence brings us back to basics, to our senses,
to our selves. It locates us. Without that return
we can go so far away from our true natures
that we end up, quite literally,
beside ourselves. We live blindly and act thoughtlessly.
We endanger the delicate balance which sustains
our lives, our communities, and our planet.

I believe that each of us can make a tremendous
difference. Politicians and visionaries will not
return us to the sacredness of life.
That will be done by ordinary men and women

who gather neighbors and friends together and say,
"Remember to breathe, remember to feel, remember to care,
remember life. Let us do this together
for ourselves and our children
and our children's children."

In this book I want to share some thoughts
about silence. I want to invite you, my neighbor,
to remember your power as a person.
I want to remind myself and others
that our homes can become sacred spaces,
filled with life and meaning.
We do not need to be experts or gurus or geniuses
to remember that all of existence is precious.
We do not need cathedrals to remind ourselves
to experience the sacred. We need only be
deeply respectful of what is fundamentally true.
And that is what we rediscover when we join in silence.

This little book, then, is offered to those
who have begun or are beginning the practice
of contemplation in silence.

11

It is for spiritual friends to use with each other
or separately. It is for any group of people
who have made a commitment to sit together.*

There are many traditions from both East and West
that teach meditation, concentration, centering,
and devotional methods. All of them are anchored
in mindfulness and silence. This primer is
a reminder of some essential attitudes and principles
which can be helpful in any meditation practice.
It is a simple tool for anyone of any tradition to use,
and is offered with reverence for all who honor
and use silence as a way.

* If you are unfamiliar with the basic concepts and procedures of group meditation,
you may wish to refer to the Afterword beginning on page 51 to get your bearings.

R o o m

When we make a place for silence, we make room
for ourselves. This is simple. And it is radical.
A room set apart for silence becomes a sanctuary
—a place for breath, for refreshment, for challenge,
and for healing. It is helpful to keep the space plain
and simple: a few cushions, a rug . . .
Simplicity allows the senses to rest from stimulation.

Silent spaces invite us to go to the inner room
—the room inside ourselves.
By making room for silence, we resist
the forces of the world which tell us to live
an advertised life of surface appearances,
instead of a discovered life—a life lived in contact
with our senses, our feelings, our deepest thoughts and values.

When a space is reserved solely for mindfulness practice,
the silence seems to deepen. A room devoted to silence
honors and invites the unknown, the untamed, the wild,

the shy, the unfathomable
—that which rarely has a chance to surface
within us. It is a visible, external symbol
of an internal reality: An actual room
signifying space within ourselves
set aside for silence.

Preparation

Before we eat a meal, we purchase food and prepare it.
Before we go on a journey, we assemble and pack
the things we need. Any activity requires preparation.
This is true for a time of silence as well.

We need a place to practice silence,
and we also need an atmosphere—a sense of harmony,
an ambiance of quiet beauty to help us on the way.

We can arrange a vase of flowers or simple greens
to soothe our eyes and help us recall
that we are part of nature, part of the order of things.

We can light a candle to ease our passage
into a different mode of being.
Perhaps it will remind us that we have inner light
to discover and share.

We can burn a stick of incense
to mark time, as Buddhist monks do:
a short stick for a half-hour of sitting,
a longer stick for forty-five minutes . . .
aromatic time. Odor reminds us
that we are sensate creatures,
that our souls live in and through our bodies.

We can strike a bell at the start of a period of sitting.
We can let the sound ring into us
—let it sound us, as in navigation, to find our depth.

Preparations like these help us to be more present
on the journey into our selves, into the world
we share in silence.

Time

A group that sits needs a time to begin

—and everyone must agree to be on time.

Starting a period of silence

and having it broken by someone's late arrival

is like the shattering of a glass.

The silence must be recovered bit by bit

and then reassembled. This takes effort.

And everyone must do it—not just the one who was late.

It is not so easy to be punctual, but it is important.

The discipline is a self-courtesy.

It teaches us to value ourselves, each other,

and the time we have been given.

To be on time we need to experience ourselves in time.

Our inner lives are timeless,

and yet our days are numbered.

To work with time we need a sense of leisure,

a sense of the natural unfolding of a day,

of a season, a year, a life.
We need also to be present to our experiences,
moment to moment. This makes for timeliness.
Then we can feel the rhythm of our lives.
Our timing becomes finer and finer.
We do not miss a beat. Leisurely and precise,
we can flow with time.

It is also helpful to allow time for the silence
to reverberate after a period of sitting.
When we are deeply touched we need time to feel.
We can dissipate what we have gained by talking
or by moving on to the next thing too quickly.
After a performance of music, there is often a quiet moment
before the audience breaks into applause. So, too,
after a period of deep sitting: Moments of quiet rest
together help us integrate what we have experienced,
easing the transition from stillness to activity.

Presence

We cannot really experience anything without being
present to it. True presence requires that we be attentive
to what is happening . . . here and now. It is an offering
of our awareness, our participation, and our willingness.
This is a basic and profound courtesy.
By such courtesy we are deeply transformed.

In silence we discover ourselves, our actual presence
to the life in us and around us. When we are present,
deeply attentive, we cannot be busy controlling.
Instead we become beholders—giving ourselves up
to the mystery of things. We become more willing
to let things be. And, as a consequence,
we can also let ourselves be.

This is so simple . . . and so hard.
Many of us have become uncomfortable with silence.
We do not regard it as a friend. In its presence
we feel uneasy, out of control.

We seek superficial reassurance for our busy minds,
instead of the deep confidence offered by
our silent vitality.

It takes time to rediscover the treasure of silence.
In it we can be found again. But we learn this
only by learning. By being present, moment to moment,
we may discern the richness of silence in ourselves
and in each other.

Sharing silence with others is a profound act of trust,
love, and courtesy. It is a mutual gift, a necessity,
a helping hand, a path, and a discipline.

Through silence our days are illumined—like rooms
filled with light—so we may inhabit our lives.

Bearing

When we sit in mindfulness practice
our backs should be straight.
Our upright posture took millions of years
to evolve. This gives our bodies an inherent dignity.

When we are upright in body we tend to be present
and alert in spirit as well. Energy can travel freely
along the spine, dancing up to the crown of the head
and down to the sacrum.

Crown and sacrum. These words hint at our worth.
When our bearing has dignity we acknowledge
the royal and sacred nature of our true selves.

Relationship

To become ourselves we need others.
Only in and through relationship do we truly become
persons. We know this from childhood.
We first learn of our existence through the eyes
of our parents. They are our first mirrors.
The process of learning who we are
—and who we might become—continues
through all the relationships of our lives.
In the deep resonance of companionship
we dare to journey to the center.

It is important to recognize how much we need
each other. This recognition removes the illusion
that we are self-created. It teaches us that giving
and taking are like inhaling and exhaling
—the breath of relationship.
By recognizing our need for each other we acknowledge
that every aspect of reality is connected to the whole,
that nothing is separate from us.

Sharing silence with another creates a bond
that cannot be compared to ordinary exchanges.
It helps us know that each of us is essential;
a vibrating essence. When we sit quietly together,
we can sense that vibration. We can feel it
singing in our cells.

When we speak, when we act, when we offer each other
food and water, we give form and expression
to the essential vibration within us. We become,
in a sense, living words. Words in combination
make complete, meaningful phrases.
Through this collaboration, potentials can be realized.
Worlds are created. In the language of life,
we are words of power.

When we support the silence in one another,
we discover what we each have been given to be.
The silence in each of us is the medium
through which the words we are may be spoken,
clearly and purely. In silence we are revealed.
This is universal and very personal.

Practice

Walking, eating a meal, dancing, breathing, chanting—
anything can be a practice as long as we are mindful,
as long as we are fully present. There are many ways,
many traditions.

To bring silence into our bodies and minds,
we must learn to be quiet. We begin by being still.
If a period of physical stillness is all we can muster,
that is enough. We have begun to practice.

If we can learn simply to follow our breath
in a steady way—attending to the inhalation
and the exhalation until we feel that we are
no longer breathing, but are being breathed
—we have grown in practice.

The point of practice is not to perform,
but to participate—not to achieve specific experiences,
but to develop a new relationship to experience itself.

25

When we no longer need to know
(or need to understand, or need to be something
other than what we are)—we are free.
We can then experience the pure unfolding of life,
the rapture of truly living. This makes happiness possible.

From the deep well of silence, joy is constantly bubbling
up and flowing out. Practice reveals that we are
immersed in that joy. Practice also reveals
what is blocking the flow.

Mutuality

When we form a group for sharing silence
it is helpful to share the leadership as well.
If only one person leads, others may become lazy,
resentful, or bored. By taking turns, we acknowledge
that all of us make up the whole.
Our responsibility is mutual. We all respond
(which originally meant to "pledge back")
by giving and receiving equitably.

When we form a group for sharing silence,
commitment to it is essential.
Our promise to each other is that we will be present
to ourselves and therefore to one another.
Together we make a holding place, much like the stones
in a well: Side by side, they make a containment
for the living water to rise through the ground,
so that anyone can draw from it.

There is no well if the stones are not steady.

As in all deep things, constancy is necessary.

Through it we become sturdy, reliable, and trustworthy,

and so find our ground water.

Mutuality and commitment—in life as in sitting,

we must give of ourselves in order to receive.

Methods

A few basic methods are helpful
in any mindfulness practice:
The first is to have a precise intention.
By focusing on one objective during a period
of meditation, we grow in concentration.

We may choose to follow our breath,
note our body's sensations, or track
the sequence of our thoughts. The objective itself
is not as important as staying with it.

The second is to be allowing—giving ourselves
to whatever comes up in the mind in relation
to our chosen objective. If we are spacious
and open-hearted to the internal flow of events,
the habitual ways in which we congeal against experience
will be broken down, releasing us into new life.

The third is to be steadfast. In returning to the practice
over and over, whether we feel like it or not, we gain
composure—no matter what
kind of experience we are having.

The fourth is to be accepting of the fact
that we cannot be flawless in our practice.
We can do what we can do.
We can be relatively still, relatively focused,
relatively allowing. Our capacity is different
in every period of silence. No matter what
our daily practice is like, however,
there is a noticeable gain over time.
If we are open to this process,
we may derive a deep sense of satisfaction
from the knowledge that we are engaged
in something larger than ourselves.
We are contacting our source.

Rhythm

Learning to be measured, to be steady in our pace,
is a process that must take place in the body.
When we strive to do things we are learning strife.
When we strain we are learning strain.
We must learn to move rhythmically, easily,
to be un-driven, to flow.

Study the way waves wash onto the shore,
or the way rings float out on a lake
when a pebble splashes through the surface
—moving without apparent effort. There is
an organic pace to this. We, too, have an organic rhythm.
Silence can help us feel it.

When we sit quietly we will sense
how long an interval of sitting is right for us.
When we practice steadily we will also know
how often to return to silence in any given day.

In our culture we do not trust time. We try to defy time.
We steal time, kill time. We want to control
the flow of events, instead of trusting
in a natural rhythm—instead of trusting
that we can and will meet life as it happens.

We attack life to defend against the mistrust
we have of ourselves. In silence we can learn
to change this. We can give ourselves time,
leaning into it, resting in it. When we do this,
the pressure comes off and we give ourselves permission
to feel and experience—because we are participating
in our lives, not controlling them. Then,
like still ponds at early dawn, we reflect
effortless effort.

Suffering

Through the practice of silence we become aware
of our pain. The pain is always there—in our minds
and in our bodies. Silence allows us to see it,
face it, release it.

We constantly judge ourselves. Our minds decide
what our experience should or should not be
—relentlessly labeling things good or bad—
and demand that our lives conform to our labels.
Then, when pain comes into our lives
—and it does to every life—we not only suffer it,
but we suffer our suffering as well.
We add the mind's harsh judgment of pain
to our actual experience of it.

By practicing silence, we may discover the ways
in which we intensify our pain by judging it.
Then we have a chance to become less harsh,
more forgiving.

The pain created by our minds is stored in our bodies,
creating rigid patterns of behavior, blocking the flow
of energy within us, cramping our being.
Our harshness and our fears are embodied in our flesh.
In silence, we can feel these tendencies harden—
and allow them to be as they are. They may then
uncramp and release, for anything that is not resisted
tends of its own accord to unfold and change.

By cultivating silence, we can find and release
deeper and deeper levels of pain and so discover
once again what is beneath the pain:
the natural joy that is already inside us,
free to rise and flow into experience.

Tendencies

The fears in our unconscious minds
create particular ways of defending
against full participation in our lives.
For whatever reason, we are each
predisposed to act and respond in certain ways.

By looking closely at these tendencies as we sit,
we may learn a great deal about ourselves.
Perhaps we will encounter chronic sleepiness,
discovering that we lack the energy
to remain awake and attentive.
Looking deeply we may find
that in our childhood we did not receive
enough attention, enough engagement,
and learned to sleep through the pain of neglect.
In silence we may slowly learn
to value and participate with ourselves.

We may find that we are measuring ourselves
against others, comparing and monitoring. Looking
deeply into childhood, we may discover
that we were asked to perform, instead of being enjoyed.
Perhaps we never had a chance to know
the pleasurable people we are. In silence
we can let this go and feel our incomparable selves.

We may feel chronic anger rising up, a hot gall.
Perhaps we were not fully heard when we were young.
We may have been shamed, or treated unjustly.
Our natural rhythms of behavior, self-discovery,
or expression may have been broken in some way,
leaving a residue of frustration in our bodies.
In silence we can learn to hear our forgotten selves,
to feel and to respond to the deep levels of our identity
that are surfacing at last.

We may discover a tremendous greed, old feelings
of having been cheated, overlooked, and dismissed.
We may actually feel the automatic impulses which are
the beginnings of our compensation for such feelings

—the compulsions that lead to overeating,
overworking, drinking, excessive sexual activity.
These compensations are meant to soothe,
to remind ourselves that we exist, but ultimately
they hurt us. In silence we can learn much about this.

We may come to realize that our habitual doubt
is a mask for self-deprecation—an unwillingness
to acknowledge what we have and what we are.
We may find that our boredom is simple laziness
—a refusal to pay attention. We may see
that our discouragement is based on false ideas
of entitlement. We think we are owed when we are not.
The lessons of silence are myriad.

In silence we have the common goal to honor
and protect our spirits. We are not being diagnostic
or prescriptive with one another. We are making
profound room in ourselves—for ourselves and
for each other. Then our tendencies can come up
as they will, one by one, and we can smile at them.
We can suffer them directly. We can slowly learn

to accept what cannot be changed . . .

and what is already whole and good within us.

In the grace of shared silence we can know

that we are imperfect and complete.

Paradox

It is a paradox that we encounter so much internal noise
when we first try to sit in silence.

It is a paradox that experiencing pain releases pain.

It is a paradox that keeping still can lead us
so fully into life and being.

Our minds do not like paradoxes. We want things
to be clear, so we can maintain our illusions of safety.
Certainty breeds tremendous smugness.

We each possess a deeper level of being, however,
which loves paradox. It knows that summer is already
growing like a seed in the depth of winter. It knows
that the moment we are born, we begin to die. It knows
that all of life shimmers, in shades of becoming
—that shadow and light are always together,
the visible mingled with the invisible.

When we sit in stillness we are profoundly active.

Keeping silent, we can hear the roar of existence.

Through our willingness to be the one we are,

we become one with everything.

Steadfastness

How do we sustain the courage and the will
to continue our practice when the going gets rough?
We know it will get rough,
and that we will encounter weariness,
frustration, and doubt.

Practicing mindfulness is much like physical training.
The long-distance runner must deal with hills
as well as valleys. The hills are hard.
And they make one strong.
If we can welcome them, and know
that they will be followed by valleys,
we will be learning something about steadfastness.

We may find the strength to continue
by taking the long view: recognizing that bliss and pain
are part of each other, that both together are more
than either is separately. Together they form reality,
the only thing that truly satisfies us.

Alternatively, we may look closely enough to see
that perseverance is also a matter of valuing
what is happening now—for its own sake.
Moment to moment, we continue by engaging fully
in the rich, dense, prolific dance of life.

Taking the long view and looking closely . . .
background and foreground.
By perseverance—through perseverance—
we become steadfast and sturdy.
We become present.

Phenomena

As we sit, we may experience many different sensations:
Our bodies may become very warm or very cold.
Our skin may become prickly and uncomfortable.
There may be a melting feeling, as if liquid gold
were coursing through us. We may see beautiful colors,
smell unusual odors. We may hear the body/mind
get stuck in old conversations, or repeating
tunes from the hit parade.

These phenomena are not of much importance.
They are not to be hungered after
or assiduously avoided. They just happen
as the body and mind begin to release
the accumulated tensions of experience.

Any phenomenon may be selected
as the object of concentration.
When one becomes especially dominant,
we have little choice but to make it our focus.

As we do this, we may discover that the phenomena
we find so compelling are not static,
but continually changing and moving and passing
on to something else.

Bit by bit, we may learn to see that everything
is impermanent, always rising or falling. We may learn
that all phenomena rest on something deeper;
something vast, endless, and timeless—our source.

Individuality

We are not static beings, and yet we are called to be
exactly who we are, unique individuals.
Our specific genetic code,
our parental influence, our education,
our friends, our work,
our whole history of experiences
—these are all the particulars through which
we have become who we are now.

When we truly acknowledge and embrace
these particulars we are making a profound contribution.
We are consciously accepting our limits,
even as they continue to change.
This is both solemn and joyful. It is what we,
as conscious beings, are asked to do—to accept
our small and unique places in this universe.

Just as water is the natural element of a fish,
our element is the vastness of life.

A fish can know water only by living in it,
swimming in it, and drawing it in through its gills.
A fish cannot know water except as a fish.
So, too, with us. We can know our true place,
our purpose, and our source only through our humanity
—by experiencing the vastness that is moving
through our small individuality. Then we will feel
intimately known, trusted, and upheld.

Passion

Because passion is an expression of love,
it encompasses suffering as well.
Love and suffering are always intertwined.

When we suffer what is truly ours to suffer, we move
into union with ourselves. We want this experience
of love, and we are afraid of it.

On some level, we know that the true meaning
of suffering is found in allowing each moment to be
what it is, remaining open to the vastness
—the life—that wants to move through us.
Where, but in silence, can we be present enough
to witness that urge of life within?

We discover these depths through silence, stillness,
and the simple act of being attentive with others.

As we enter into exquisite awareness of the life that wants to live *as us*, we learn to love deeply. We claim our passion.

Peace

Peace is not absence of strife. Peace is acceptance
and surrender to that which is. Peace is
the profound awareness of the one true source
from which all things emerge . . .
and to which all things return.

However lost we may feel, we are never outside
of the source. We are intimately known by it,
sustained by it, and returned to it—daily . . . now . . .
and when we pass away. The source delights in us,
becomes in us, plays in us.

When we contact the source, our practice
has led us to the end and to the beginning.
Then we can be at peace—for no matter what occurs
in our lives, we can always find our way home
to the core, the truth of our being.

Afterword

There are countless ways of sharing silence with others: daily practice, weekly practice, longer retreats . . . sitting with friends, family, or more formally organized groups . . . simply sitting in silence, with no structure at all . . . working with images, with sound, with movement . . . employing any of the various forms of mindfulness practice, which may involve all of our senses, our thinking and feeling. Many books are readily available from which you may learn more about any of these approaches.

The basic procedures of a period of meditation (or a *sit*) are wonderfully simple: Select a room. Put some cushions on the floor. Sit on them. Each period of sitting may last from thirty minutes to an hour or more. A single period of perhaps forty-five minutes, once a week, is a good first goal (though you may wish to begin with thirty minutes until everyone can comfortably sit for longer periods).

Later you may wish to move on to occasional all-day sits, consisting of five or more sessions of varying lengths, with ten-minute "intermissions," an hour for lunch (ideally without conversation), and one or two "walking meditations" (in which one person leads the others on a slow and mindful walk, in silence, indoors or out). The groups which inspired this book have chosen to sit once a week for an hour and once a month for a day. The sits are always held in the same room, which is not used for any other purpose. Generally the leadership is shared.

As a discipline, we select a topic which will be our focus of contemplation over the course of several months. These topics are always "large" and simple, such as *trust, simplicity, compassion, or community*.

Our periods of silence often begin with a few minutes of spoken reflection by that day's leader. Though group leaders are encouraged to speak in their own words, some prefer not to. In that case, there are many excellent books from which to read aloud. Here are a few favorites:

Tao Te Ching: A New English Version with Foreword and Notes by Stephen Mitchell (HarperCollins).

The poems of the Sufi mystic, Rumi, translated by John Moyne and Coleman Barks. Some titles are: *These Branching Moments* (Copper Beech Press), *We Are Three* (Maypop Books), *Open Secret* and *Unseen Rain* (Threshold Books).

Zen Mind, Beginner's Mind by Shunryu Suzuki, (Weatherhill). *The Miracle of Mindfulness* (Beacon Press) and *Being Peace* (Parallax Press) by Thich Nhat Hanh.

One might ask: Why read or speak at all if the point is to be together in silence? My answer would be that words can both grow out of silence and bring us to it. The discursive, conceptual mind is always at work. By giving it something to work with, we allow our non-conceptual mind—the *being* part of us—to sink deep into the well of silence and breathe the mystery of what always is and can never be named.

After the leader has spoken, a bell is rung to signify the start of silence and the beginning of meditation. How we sit is a private matter: Some of us close our eyes, some keep them open but unfocused. Though sitting cross-legged and straight-backed is recommended, some of us prefer to sit with legs outstretched or to use a kneeling bench. At the designated time, with some allowance for an intuitive sense of the right moment, the bell is rung again to conclude the sit. After resting quietly for a short while, we share whatever thoughts and impressions we wish to pass along to each other.

Mindfulness practice is greatly enriched by the discipline of sustaining concentration for extended periods—a whole day, a week, a month. A good resource book to help structure such experiences is *Silence, Simplicity and Solitude: A Guide for Spiritual Retreat* by David A. Cooper (Bell Tower). It has a fine overview of the major spiritual traditions and a good bibliography, as well as sample schedules for days of meditative retreat.

If a sitting group remains stable through months and years, deep communion and trust grow, along with the capacity to dwell in silence for longer and longer periods of time. Through this process, we are fundamentally changed and begin to participate in the peace that lies beyond understanding.

Acknowledgments

My deep gratitude goes to Greta D. Sibley for the generous and unfailing attention she has given to this project and for her design of a limited edition of the book published by Small Offerings Press. In addition, I want to thank Norman Sibley for his superb editorial help in the limited edition publication of this book.

My appreciation to my editor at Bell Tower, Toinette Lippe, for her faithful encouragement and support.

And lastly, my gratitude to everyone who has deeply participated in the shared silences that inspired and sustained the writing of this book.

Becoming Bread

Meditations on Loving and Transformation

Drawings by John Giuliani

This book is dedicated to the source of all relation-ships, with gratitude for Jennifer, John, Dobritte, and Chloe, treasured friends, and in memory of Lee, who shared his bread with grace.

Contents

Acknowledgments

Many thanks to Toinette Lippe, not only for her skill as an editor but also for her longtime dedication to publishing spiritually useful books. I want to thank my son, John, and the following friends for thoughtfully responding to the manuscript in whole or in part: Platt Arnold, Lee Brunner, Carolyn Dukenski, Danit Freid, Greg Johanson, Ro King, Howard Lawrence, Florence Phillips, Greta Sibley, Norman Sibley, Joyce Sievers, Gail Straub, and Ellen Wingard. My thanks also to my agent, Bob Silverstein, for his encouragement. I want to give additional thanks to Greta Sibley, whose wonderful design ideas have helped me "see" the book. And my gratitude to Marjorie Anderson, who did the final graceful design, and to John Giuliani for his lovely drawings.

Preface

For a long time I have wanted to write a book about loving. I have wanted to do this as a continuing question—an inquiry really, because good questions sometimes carry answers on their backs.

Love for me has been a powerful question . . . one asked even more penetratingly after my marriage of twenty-eight years ended. In those years I loved much and so did my husband. Yet the relationship ended. I have loved family and friends and I have been loved by them. Some of these relationships have reached depths I could not have dreamed of. Grace became visible and changed me forever. Other relationships have stayed on the surface, pleasantly skipping along like flat stones. And some have been devastating.

Why is this? Why is love so nourishing and yet so painful? How can it be everywhere? How can it also be so elusive? What can we say about it? Love—so varied, so strange, and so common. How do we receive this gift?

Perhaps we cannot rightly love each other or ourselves unless we love God. Perhaps the truth is that we cannot love God unless we love ourselves and each other. Is love ever understood except through experience? I don't know how to answer these questions. But they feel life-giving to me. And I want to spend the rest of my life trying to find the answers to them.

To ask is to question as well as to request, to claim, to expect, to need, and to call for. This book is part of my asking and I hope you will join me with your asking. I think we have all felt that we become more fully ourselves when we love and are loved. We know that love nourishes us. When it is in our lives, we can bear pain, confusion, and even death. This is why I link the food of the spirit, love, and the food of the body, bread. Both are staples. They sustain us.

Beginning

Bread on a journey is no burden.

Russian proverb

We do not need to own a kitchen or spend time in one to know the significance of bread. We need never see a bread recipe or try our hand at baking to realize that bread is a profound and ancient symbol for life. To grow grain and to store it guaranteed our ancestors the possibility of survival. The oldest grain cereal known to man was the common wheat native to the prehistoric plains of Asia. It was cultivated by the Stone Age man of the Neolithic period. Here was the beginning of bread.

Flour and salt—the makings of bread—were frequently brought to our early altars. The sacrifices were made in recognition of the fact that we are fundamentally creatures of need. These offerings were petitions for sustenance. We have understood from the beginning how dependent and vulnerable we are. We have known that in order to live we will always have to receive and care for the gifts of life.

And we have also known that we must share these gifts. They are not for us alone. Hoarded, they molder just as uneaten bread molders. We must share life, share bread with each other. We are each given only so much time. And to make this time matter, in order to really live, we need to give, we need to receive. We need to love. Bread, life, and love are fused in the soul of human experience.

Our religious and philosophical texts are filled with references to bread, and proverbs about it abound in our folk wisdom. Holidays and family events are marked by the eating of festive breads to commemorate these special moments. We share bread at almost every meal, forgetting how old this is in us.

Deep in our souls we know that *we* are the bread of life and that to become conscious of this and to live it makes all the difference ... it frees us to be more truly human and to care for each other.

Becoming Bread is a book of meditations for sharing with someone we love and cherish. It asks the reader to see the steps of making bread as the unfolding process of self-knowledge, of growing communion with a loved one, and of surrender to the huge context in which we dwell. None of this can be hurried, just as making bread cannot be hurried.

When a loaf of bread is taken out of the oven, it is hot and moist. It is laid on the breadboard and the kitchen fills with yeasty fragrance. Much has happened for this bread to have come into being. And more will continue to happen.

We smell the bread. We see its brown patina and touch the crust. Warmth comes into our fingertips. We experience the bread as we do our loving . . . with all of our senses. To be here, on the breadboard, this loaf has gone through the fire. Soon it will be consumed and give nourishment. And soon it will also be forgotten.

When we look at the loaf we may think how we, too, must go through fire to become ourselves, to become sustenance for each other and for life itself. We are each part of this mystery. This is how life has always been, how it has manifested itself in the universe— becoming, sustaining, and surrendering to become again another way, another time.

Love. Bread. It breaks. It crumbles. It nourishes. We share it. Bread that comes from grain, from earth, from rain, from summer and light, from labor and threshing. Bread of comfort, of necessity, of sorrow. Bread that brings life. Fresh bread. Stale bread. Bread crumbs. We are all of that.

The potential for a loving relationship with ourselves, with each other, and with God is a gift. We cannot *make* it. But we can choose to be oriented toward the only place loving can occur, namely right here, now, where we are. Just the living of that orientation makes it more possible for this gift, this blessing, to happen to us and for us to receive it. Each time we share bread with each other, we symbolize this mystery.

Perhaps only sages can truly speak about loving and how it transforms us. We are not sages. We are ordinary people. I hope that this ordinariness will be a good enough credential to entitle any of us to speak from the heart. And to speak boldly even as we know that we do not really know. For here, together, we are becoming, becoming something which is not yet apparent. Dough does not know what is being made of it. Yet bread possesses an absolute integrity. Perhaps we can accept that unknowing is a blessing, for then we can be transformed, we can become something "for God."

Place

The field is God's table.

Estonian proverb

Making bread is as mysterious as loving and yet it is something anyone can do. To make bread we know we need some kind of kitchen. To love we know we must meet each other *somewhere*. We know that place of meeting is none other than the here and now. There is no meeting anywhere else. We cannot live separately from what is.

We are given bodies. We are given the world. We are given time. But without attention, without awareness, without true presence, we do not meet, we do not find each other. There is no "kitchen."

In the here and now dwells the truth that all of us are limited . . . that we are continuously moving and changing . . . always longing and reaching for the not-yet. The truth is that we are the energy in these bodies, burning through time . . . that we are dying. This is fundamental—our earth, our water, our air, and our fire.

Let us meet where we already are, in the elements of our vulnerability. In this we are together and we cannot do without each other. This is basic. Our neighbor is our self.

The Kitchen

Familiar and strange,
the kitchen is a holy place—
alive with possibility.

A place for the elements.
Water in the tap,
fire in the stove,
earth in the food,
air—between, around, above, and below.

Behind the cupboard doors
are the pots and the pans,
the bowls and the dishes,
the measuring cups
and the measuring spoons—

holy things
that lie ready for use,
much like our dreams
that lie waiting
behind our eyelids.

The kitchen is alchemical,
a place where we cook—actually
and spiritually. We come to it
for nourishment and ease.
We come to it as to a center—

the heart of the house,
the heart of dwelling.
In the kitchen we are one,
linked by hunger—
actual hunger and spiritual hunger.

We go to the kitchen to be
nourished and revealed.
It is a holy place.

At the Threshold

Stand at the kitchen door with me.
Honor the heart of transformation.
Honor your own heart
where everything is
always changing.
It is the very same dwelling.

Pause at the door.
Your heart needs this.
My heart needs this time
for recognition or it will go astray.
It will forget to reach for
its real joy . . . its true becoming.

Pause at the door.
This is good and necessary
for this room is *every* room.
The world lives here.
Pausing each day helps us know
nothing is outside of us.

Honor the heart that can feel
the joy and the terror of
the world in you and in me.
Only what is truly human
can walk this path, walk through
and be constant. Bow to *that* heart.

Hold my hand. I need you for courage.
We become who we are together,
each needing the other. Alone is a myth.
The path leads through this door.
I cannot go to the kitchen without you.
Let us enter together.

Willingness

Hunger teaches us many things.

Irish proverb

Not only do we need a kitchen to bake bread, we need the will to be engaged in the process. This is true of loving also. Without the will to love, we cannot be consistent. "Love is a direction and not a state of the soul," as Simone Weil says.

But there is a tension here, for will can as easily be willful as it can be willing. And there is a vast difference between the two. Most often willfulness is based on fear. We try to make the world the way we want it by forcing solutions. Compensating for the uncertainty inside us, we become motivated by power instead of participation. Then we find struggles instead of solutions because force is often met with resistance. We stay emotionally hungry yet cannot be fed. We ask for more and more, and receive less. Willingness, on the other hand, allows life to show us the way.

"Thy will be done," we say in the Lord's Prayer. And the very next line is, "Give us this day our daily bread." Truly prayed, this is a prayer of willingness . . . willingness to desire God's will. Willingness to feel and recognize hunger and therefore willingness to receive sustenance. Willingness to forgive and be forgiven. This prayer understands our human nature.

When we can open the cupboard door in the heart's kitchen, we are expressing this acceptance of creatureliness. As we look at the ingredients inside . . . the ones we like and the ones we prefer to deny . . . we are beginning to trust God to make bread out of all that. The outcome won't be up to us, but we will be participating. We will begin to "intend to make the service of love a beautiful thing," as the twelfth-century Beguine, Hadewijch of Antwerp, tells us, "Want nothing else, fear nothing else, and let love be free to become what love truly is."

Water

In this heart place there is order
and disorder. Riptides. Storms
and dead calm. Here in the kitchen
we find a sea of unknown feelings.

We are born in these waters.
We bear each other in them.
Beginning again . . . like waves . . .
outgoing . . . incoming . . .
orderless order . . . deep water.

This place is innocent and wild.
It is our own moods and weather
we find here. When I am calm, you are
orderless. When you sort, I disorganize.

We cannot reassure each other
in these storms. Between the counters
there is foul weather and what we have
relied on in each other floats away.

Finding love here in the outgoing . . .
incoming tide . . . we must begin again
to trust and so take up unknowing
as a way, a truthful pattern.

We bear ourselves for the sake of the other.
We bear the other for the sake of ourselves.
The truth we have not dared to live yet
deepens here . . . fathomless water.

The Mixing Bowl

Here on the table
is the mixing bowl.
Brown and ordinary,
turned on the potter's wheel,
it has an umber rim
and glazed, cinnamon-speckled sides.

Its task is to be open,
a simple space. This bowl is
clay, earth, matter. Particular.
We are like it. Clay,
earth, matter. Particular
and vast when we are empty . . .

when life can fill us
to the rim, brimming.
We are the mixing place
where terror and hate,
where love and hope,
the way we move,

our smiles and uncertainties,
our courage and stupidities
are all embraced.
We are the body bowl . . .
the forming space,
the home of possibility.

Hunger

In this place hunger is our guide.
What shall we find here to nourish us?
We have nothing of our own . . .
nothing but need.

I forage for the pans.
You bring out the bowl.
The cups gape—wide
like open mouths. Hungry.

These things are empty.
Let us be like them . . . begging
to be filled. This hunger is our gift.
The one we want

to look away from. The one we hide
from one another. Let me learn
to love you in your want. I beg you
to love the hunger that is mine.

Do not seek to allay it. Do not be afraid.
Protect my hunger with love
for then I shall find the way to become
real bread. And you shall be fed.

Discover the grain that hides in your hunger,
the one that can be worked into a loaf,
and I shall feast on your joy.
Light a light so that we see the emptiness

of the pot and the pan, the emptiness
in the curve of the spoon, the emptiness
in the shape of your hand that can cradle
my hunger and yet not take it from me.

In this gift of sheltering I will find
that my hunger is life hungering for itself
and that I can trust that hunger, receive it
as my truth, as myself.

Bowls and cups, pots and pans,
spoons—my hand, your hand.
We shall come to know ourselves
as vessels that can hold this moment

for each other, for the greater life
that seeks itself in us, trusts us and
hungers in us. Let us be vessels . . .
openings . . . sheltering space.

Seeing

"Bread," we say,
looking at one another. "Bread,"
we say, looking at ourselves.

There is flour in the cupboard,
salt, and honey—the ingredients
of bread on the shelves. Here

I may find what I was afraid to see.
Here you may see what you didn't know
you had. The risk of knowing

is here in the cupboard. . . .
How little we have dared to use ourselves.
How much has been kept from each other.

"Bread," we say. "Let me see
inside the cupboard. Let me
look behind the door."

I am afraid when you can see
what I would not look at
for then I must know myself.

On the shelf the sack
we call flour might be empty,
might be full of miller moths—unusable.

On the shelf there might be
bounty—sacks and sacks of wheat,
and I could feel the shame of riches,

a terrible abundance that could tear us
apart. Make a rift. You poor . . . me rich
and therefore both in poverty.

I am afraid when you see
what I would not look at.
Your eyes are my witness.

If they look with love
I can bear to see what I have to offer—
the grain of my experience . . . my flour.

Gifts

You can think as much as you like
but you will invent nothing better
than bread and salt.

Russian proverb

To make bread we have to take the ingredients out of the cupboard and assemble them so they can be seen and used. We have to know and understand what is there.

What *is* there? The earth under our feet. The water in our glasses. The simple tastes of sweet and salt. The seasons. The very rhythm of life. The list can go on. We are grounded in these basic gifts.

We do not appreciate these gifts unless we recognize them . . . and recognize them repeatedly. They are the manna, the daily bread from heaven. New each day. To be used each day. "Be ready at all times for the gifts of God and always for new ones," says Meister Eckhart. They are given to us even if we don't receive them. They are the continual ingredients of our lives.

But when we do receive them, when we honor the goodness around us, we sense that we are released from our narrow self-absorbed view. A midrash tells us that "when the world was created God made everything a little bit incomplete. Rather than making bread grow right out of the earth, God made wheat grow so that we might bake it into bread. In this way we could become partners in completing the work of creation."

Recognition. Repetition. Reverence. Receiving. These are ways we grow to know that we ourselves are integral parts of the whole. We, too, are manna.

Spring

We open the bags.
The flour lies there
soft and brown—grain
we can touch—grain
we can smell and use.

The wheat has Spring in it.
Even now it contains
those early plantings, the growth
reaching forward into time,
into a future harvest—this flour.

I want to remember your Spring
as constant . . . as here in this wheat.
I want to think of you young.
I want to think of me beginning . . .
both of us reaching into earth,

into the future, rooting into life,
where we meet now—where we are
asking for nourishment . . . asking
to become bread for one another. As we sift
this fine flour I want to feel you greening.

Earth

Your wheat grew in the ground as did mine.
We have no experience without soil.
Background—our parents and their parents.
Home-ground—our feet on this earth.

Made from ground, sustained by ground,
we are soil. This is the first humility.
If we forget this, we forget that we are human.
We are of the land. We are humus.

Measuring

Made of glass, the measuring cup
is transparent. It holds and it measures
as in music. There is a rhythm here—
a rightness . . . something tempered.

It is not good for a melody to rush
beyond its tempo. So, too, in bread.
The water must be measured.
Two cups and a little more.

One for you and one for me
and some for the stranger . . .
the one we do not know in ourselves.
Pour the water . . . the living measure

into the mixing bowl—love's alembic.
Not too much. Not too little. Let it fall.
Let it seek its level. Let it run from the well,
into the bowl . . . sufficient to the heart.

Salt

Add the salt. A tablespoon of flavor.
Salt from the sea. Salt from the mountain.
Salt from the body . . .
salt after our tears have dried . . .
the residue of grief and frustration.
In time this salt will preserve us.

Add the salt after sweat,
after effort. What our work has
asked of us again and again.
Over time this salt will preserve us
and our memory of movement . . .
our memory of engagement.

Add the salt after running,
after play, after the joy of games.
Add the salt after sex,
after the mystery of union. . . .
Add this body salt, this life salt.
Dissolve it in the bowl, in water.

Summer

Let the golden honey run
out of the jar. Let the water
be sweetened in our mixing bowl.

Three giant spoonfuls
of Summer—nectar, sunshine,
the hum of bees, warm nights,

and ourselves in the grass.
Three giant spoonfuls of Summer
sweetening the water in the mixing bowl.

We need this liquid gold
to remember the goodness
of life . . . the taste of honey.

The memory of Summer . . .
that it returns, that at the center
the open flower is sweet.

That at the center
when it opens, we too are sweet,
and love, like a swarm of bees,

can fly into us . . . ecstatic,
nectar-drunk and
powdered with pollen.

Our bread will have this
poured-from-the-center
rich gold . . . three giant spoonfuls.

Yeast

When the yeast is added
we will see in the honey water
the unpredictable, the alive . . .
which we can never own or
truly understand. We will see
how it bubbles and froths—
how it rises up—and we will know
that we do not have control. . . .

When the yeast is added
to the sweet and the salty,
the skin-temperature,
warm-blooded water, we will sense
the irrepressible and how it moves
into the very cells of our bodies,
into the blood and marrow. We are
flesh and we are vulnerable. . . .

When the yeast is added—
the impulsive, the unmanageable,
the free—we know we will be
moved. Every part of the mixture!
The inert lump of dough will come alive,
will expand and yield. We will be lifted
out of ourselves, beyond ourselves.
We will be worked. . . .

Autumn

The flour in the sack is soft—
a powdered silk. It is beautiful.
It has become this way
because it was harvested, because
it was threshed, and then milled.

Here is the terror of Autumn.
And the beauty! What is ripe *is*
sacrificed. Torn loose. The grain
is wrested from the plant, from everything
familiar. We must expect this to happen

to ourselves. I want to know this in you . . .
that you have been on the threshing floor.
I need you to see that I have been
between the grinding stones. It will make us
careful of each other, of all grain.

The flour in the sack is soft—
a powdered silk. How terrible is beauty.
How full of sacrifice and grace.
Let us honor all that has dared
to grow to fruition.

Living

The crop of the field is always rich in hope.

Spanish proverb

Once the ingredients are assembled, once they are mixed together into a dough, they will become part of each other. They will be one thing. Life . . . becoming bread . . . becoming life.

Process. We can smile at the pictures we have of it in our minds. Still lives—particular moments in their gilded frames. And yet we know experience is something else. It moves! And we are in it.

In a single day there are thousands of changes. We are confused by them, delighted by them, upset by them, dreaming toward them, rejecting them, longing for them, making predictions for the future about them. We live in our thoughts instead of our lives. If we were truly living we would experience what Pierre Teilhard de Chardin wrote: that "by matter we are nourished, lifted up, linked to everything else, invaded by life."

There is no other way than presence and engagement, participation and compassion. Loving the whole, learning as we go, living as we live. "Once you know how the dough becomes bread, you will understand enlightenment," said Shunryu Suzuki, Roshi. We have to be willing to be dough in order to become bread. There is no other way.

Mixing Dough

Now the flour is added.
Watch it start to be
absorbed in the sweet and salty
water, the yeast-milky water.

Watch the critical moment
when suddenly there is a shift.
Now the flour begins
to absorb the water. God's love

works this way. At first
we are dissolved in it
and then we begin to absorb it
. . . becoming substantial.

We do not know how this happens.
Turned, mixed, and stretched,
made pliable. God-infused,
we are asked to be dough.

On the Counter

Taken out, exposed
on the counter,
I am being kneaded.

The air pounded
out of me,
I am turned

inside out. Rolled over
as if by a breaker.
Beached . . .

I am in the open.
Do not leave me now.
Do not hurt me

or give advice.
Do not rescue me.
Do not stop this.

It is my true chance.
Upside down I may
take shape. I may become

more of myself,
resilient. Let this happen.
Here on the counter

kneaded, turned on end
I will become *less*
and somehow more myself.

Hold my hand.
Do nothing. Soon
it may happen. Soon

I may be kneaded into shape,
smooth, all of one piece,
able to dream forward again.

Soon you may join me
here on the counter.
And I will know you as myself.

Rising

Here in the bowl
is warmth and time to rest.
The dough is set apart and covered.

Here in the bowl
the rising starts
and creeps up the sides

reaching into time,
into space . . . into possibility.
Dreams are like this,

full of air,
going ahead of us,
wanting to take us

beyond the rim
of our horizon,
wanting to lift us out

of where we are.
Dreams are like this . . . unfolding
a moment at a time,

expanding us, breathing us,
demanding something new,
wanting to take shape.

This is also dangerous
for there are dark dreams, terrible
dreams. And the ones where

love asks the impossible from us.
Can this be the restlessness
of God? Are we being dreamed?

Discipline

Live within your harvest.

Persian proverb

After the dough is mixed and kneaded, it grows light with air. Slowly the yeast does its work and the dough rises in the bowl to be punched down and kneaded again. Then it is divided and the bread pans are filled. The dough rises a second time in the individual pans.

We must work with time and with patience if we want to make bread. There is no point in making it if we do not accept this. This is true of loving also.

Awareness . . . acceptance . . . patience. It takes everything we have to be able to live this way. It means that we finally take up what is ours to do and let go of what is beyond our abilities. Life corrects us if we do not learn this. As Montaigne put it, "Greatness of soul consists not so much in soaring high and in pressing forward, as in knowing how to adapt and limit oneself." Einstein was more wry. He said, "The only rational way of educating is to be an example—if one can't help it, a warning example." These lessons cannot be skipped. They are rigorous and yet ultimately kind.

Our natures have organic rules that are innate and God-given. To live by those rules is essential—a discipline, a necessity. Perhaps a better word is *obedience*. No one can tell us how to obey our natures except our natures. It takes self-control . . . a profound way of attending to our deepest truth. Can we love each other this way? Can we give each other time and awareness? Can we help each other listen? Can we help each other hear?

Punching Down

To think we know the dream God has
placed in us . . . to think we know
how to make it happen. . . . Let this be
punched down. Let this be the Winter blow.

God trusts us—fills our lungs, fills
our bodies, fills our lives. We are God's
dough. If we think this is our doing,
let the punch come—the Winter blow.

God trusts us—fills our cells, fills
our thoughts, moves with our gestures.
If we believe this is our doing,
let the punch come—the Winter blow.

So profoundly does God trust us,
we are asked to return trust with trust,
with true unknowing. A Winter faith,
a blessed darkness where God is at rest

in us. Where we can be at rest in God.
All separation gone. Punch down all
but this enjoyment . . . living without
a why. Living *with* living—a Winter faith.

On the Counter Again

Taken out, exposed
and cold on the counter,
you are being kneaded.

The air pounded
out of you,
you are turned

inside out. Rolled over
in waves.
Everything made visible

on the counter.
I will not leave you now.
I will not hurt you

or give advice.
I will not rescue you.
I will not stop this.

It is your true chance.
Upside down you may
take shape. You may become

more of yourself,
resilient. Let this happen.
Here on the counter

pounded, turned on end.
You will become *less*
and somehow more yourself.

I hold your hand
and do nothing. Soon
it may happen.

You will be kneaded
into shape, smooth,
able to go on again.

We are together here
on the counter and alone.
You will know me as *yourself*.

Shaping

No sooner complete
than incomplete—
All of a piece—then divided.
Torn in half—in thirds and quarters.

To become a loaf
the dough must be given shape.
Set apart. Torn apart.

We must bear this process,
the separation, the aloneness,
the truth that we are singular.
We cannot escape ourselves.

This is suffering
which must be borne or it will be
borne by others . . . more dreadfully.

We are revealed in our solitude
and look at the world
from that place, that vastness. . . .
Your eyes tell me you are infinite.

Limits

The pans are ready.
Their metal edges gleam.
They are greased and floured.
They are ready to hold *just so much* dough.

There is nothing personal here.
This restriction must happen
the way death must happen.
It *is* the way.

Our lives depend on limits.
Our skins first. Our parents—
just those two. Our homes.
Our loves, our work, our friends.

Our talents and our appalling lacks.
Our very breath. In. Out.
The lungs' capacity. No more.
Only so much can be lived!

The pans have limits,
and the dough will grow within them.
This is dependable and good.
A mercy.

The Second Rising

God longs for God
and uses us,
rises in us . . .
becomes in us.

Let us be silent,
a quiet dough

where God moves
into every pore . . .
where God lives
as God pleases.

Let us rise simply.
A quiet dough.

Pain

Bread is relief for all kinds of grief.

Spanish proverb

The dough is put in the oven. Our lives are put to the test. The heat is on. Simone Weil tells us, "When an apprentice gets hurt, or complains of being tired, the workmen and peasants have this fine expression: 'It is the trade entering his body.' Each time that we have some pain to go through, we can say to ourselves quite truly that it is the universe, the order and beauty of the world, and the obedience of creation of God that are entering our body."

Yet the fire can seem unbearable. Feelings burn hot and so very precisely. The place where we hurt the most is also where the greatest possibilities lie. Pain wakes us up.

When those we love are in the fire and we can only watch, it is terrible. We feel helpless and afraid. When we are in the fire and no escape is possible, we tremble and shrink back. The passage through and into the heat of life is what we want . . . what we dread. "Who never ate his bread with tears, who never sat weeping on his bed during care-ridden nights knows you not, you heavenly powers," said Goethe.

Yet our pains can and do begin to heal in the cauterizing flame, in the heat of becoming. We wait with those we love when they are there. We try to trust their pain and ours. Can we bear it? Can we somehow let it have its way?

Fire

In the oven. In the pitch black
of the heat, of the sealed fire.
In the oven we are taken
out of ourselves,
into the unbearable . . .

that place where
all hope dies, where
dreams are stunned
out of existence.
Heat. No thought possible.
No breath. No help.

No direction known.
No rescue available.
Nothing but fire.
It is what we are,
what we become. Nothing.
God's heat or nothing.

Waiting

In this darkness
the minutes shrink us,
the seconds dry us out.

Time is an enemy.
When will this suffering be over?
When will it finish?

You are there, helpless.
My hand goes out
but does not bring relief.

I am there, helpless.
Your eyes fill with tears
and you cannot help me.

The pain lives in us.
It is our particular pain.
Necessary pain. We wait on it.

When will it be done?
When will it be finished?
The minutes bake us.

Dry time, mini-seconds,
time-as-it-ticks-time.
It forges us.

We wait on it and long
for God's time—
Time within time.

Standing Free

The knife scrapes along
the metal edge of the pan.
The bread moves.

It is free. And yet
it holds its shape.
This is a mystery.

Brown and fragrant,
the limits are within it now.
The loaf can stand on its own.

In this way we become
ourselves also. Able to stand.
Free. Together. And alone.

This is a mystery.
We find ourselves *here*
side by side. Warm. Newly born.

Sharing

Even crumbs are bread.

Danish proverb

We are united through sharing . . . our lives made meaningful . . . made new. "Take. Eat. This is my body," said Jesus when He broke the bread at the Last Supper. Then He gave His life for us. Behind all communion is the knowledge that we must give our lives to each other, for each other.

And when we do, we can celebrate, we can mourn, we can trust, we can forgive, we can treasure, we can face our deaths. By sharing we are transformed and come to understand with Meister Eckhart that "all bread is *ours* and is given to me, to others through me, and to me through others. For not only bread but all things necessary for sustenance in this life are given on loan to us with others and to others through us."

In sharing, the meaning of our lives is given back to God.

> The One who gives.
> The One who receives.
> The One who is.

Cooling

So close to the heat,
to the transforming fire,
the bread must now rest.
The loaves need to breathe

on the cooling rack.
They fill the air
with their fragrance,
with the smell of

comfort, the recollection
that there is sometimes plenty,
that we will be nourished,
and that we, too, are food.

We can meet now.
We can come together
to nourish and to receive,
to break bread.

Texture

Hold the bread in your hand—
feel its texture—the integrity of it!

Take the bread in your hand,
and then give it away. Give

the crunch of the crust, and
the softness of the center.

Give the hardness of the heel,
and the crispness of the crumbs.

Give it all. This is life which nourishes
as we give it all away.

Breaking Bread

Break the loaf.
See the miracle
that the bread
springs back at you!

Light and full of air.
Held together with earth
and water. Warmed with fire.
Moist and fragrant.

Receive this bread
and break it.
It is you.
It is me.

It is us together.
It is whole.
It is broken.
Receive this bread.

Crumbs

Be careful with the crumbs.
Do not overlook them.

Be careful with the crumbs:
the little chances to love,

the tiny gestures, the morsels
that feed, the minims.

Take care of the crumbs:
a look, a laugh, a smile,

a teardrop, an open hand. Take care
of the crumbs. They are food also.

Do not let them fall.
Gather them. Cherish them.

Plenty

Having shared our bread,
we know that we are
no longer hungry. It is enough

that you see me for myself.
That I see you for yourself.
That we bless what we see

and do not borrow, do not use
one another. This is how we know
we are no longer hungry . . . that

the world is full of terror, full of beauty
and yet we are not afraid to find solace here.
To be bread for each other. To love.

Savoring

God's hand is always opening.

Spanish proverb

To take nothing for granted and to receive much, this changes everything, makes us empty, makes us new. It transforms us. All gratitude comes from this, that we truly *receive* our lives, each other, and the world.

Time and space. Air and fire. Earth and water. The hot and the dry. Spring and Summer. The cold and the moist. Fall and Winter. Sight. Sound. Touch and smell. Mercy. Terror. Limitation. Pain. When we receive all of it, the whole of life's beauty . . . it *is* bread . . . it is love and we can pray the ancient prayer, "Holy One of Blessing, Your Presence fills creation, bringing forth bread from the earth."

Being human and ordinary, we will often fail to love the whole, the dark and difficult parts. We will always try to avoid something. We will tremble. We will be blind. We will be uncertain. We will continue to hurt one another and miss the essential. We will always need mercy and compassion. We will be ineffective, stubborn, and very human. It is ultimately our vulnerability and our powerlessness that God loves the most, I believe. For there we can and do receive, *must receive*, and know that everything is a gift. Even our suffering.

Full of that knowledge, that sustenance, we cannot help but share our love and our lives with each other. Then we are not only becoming bread . . . we *are* bread.

Beginning Again

Here is the kitchen.
Will you enter it with me?
Let us share the heart of the house.

Here dwelling and becoming
are like angels to wrestle with.
Here limitation will be our friend

and we can grow into love,
into bread. You, a sustenance for me,
and I, a sustenance for you.

Both of us fostered by
the measuring cup, shaped by
the teaspoon and the quarter-teaspoon.

Here the shining world grows
more transparent in its beauty each day.
We are disappearing in its light,

turning into the moment's bright copper,
surrendering to what we do not know
. . . what we cannot see or touch.

Here is the kitchen. Here let us become
the very nourishment we long for.
Becoming what we *are*, unknowing,

light, praise, shared bread. . . .
A living way.

Journeying in Place

Reflections from a Country Garden

Drawings by Susan Mangam

Mother was a constant beholder and appreciator of color and form. She could often be seen in small raptures at scenes and figures that impressed her. As a painter and tapestry designer she had individual exhibits in Portugal, Sweden, the United States, and Venezuela, as well as participating in many group shows. She was the winner of the Prix d'une Artiste Etrangère, the Salon des Femmes Peintres, and the Grand Prix International Clermont-Ferrand. Even on the very last day of her life, I saw her sketching on the inside of a book of matches.

She married my father, Gunnar Daniel Dryselius, in 1935 and served with him in the Swedish diplomatic corps until he retired as ambassador to Portugal. Their tours of duty took them to Czechoslovakia, Poland, Argentina, the United States, Venezuela, and ultimately Portugal.

She had three children: my sister, Anita; myself, Gunilla; and my brother, Jan. She was the grandmother of Bradford, Emily, Faith, Hillary, Jennifer, John, and Susanna.

A splendid-looking woman with much energy, she lived a full, dynamic life. Anna Christina was loved and is sorely missed. This book honors her.

Contents

All Saints' Day

I found my mother dead in the early morning on this day a year ago. All Saints' Day. In the Christian church calendar it is the day when the departed are celebrated and remembered. In the old Celtic and Anglo-Saxon calendars it is the day when the new year begins, first of November. The killing frost has happened both in my garden and in my life. I have lost my mother. The harvest has been gathered. The light has changed. The new year is at hand.

My farming ancestors took this season as an opportunity to begin again. When the fields were harvested and the soil turned, when the ground was frozen and the trees had lost their leaves, they were freed from their usual labors. Time could be spent in other ways, in storytelling, in fellowship, in preparing and repairing, in planning and reflecting, in remembering. I follow in their footsteps.

I want to go into memory now, to harvest my experiences and to share them. I want to make a journey through the landscape where I live, a journey *in place,* a journey through nature's year. Journey is really too active a word, for it implies a distance traveled from here to there. I do not mean that. I mean instead a circling in time, remembering a year as if it were all years. It is a way for me to honor my mother, experiencing the living of each season in celebration of her who gave me life.

For me recalling the seasons and the small particulars of my life is something like developing photographs. I have lived with a certain perspective, in very specific moments of time. They are my inner snapshots. Whether I am aware of it or not, the film has been exposed and developed. It holds my memory. Now the prints lie in the pan of developing fluid. What they really are is not yet known to me. But slowly, as they rise, I can see shapes take form. There is light and there is dark. I begin to see outlines, and when the prints finally float to the surface I see images reflecting my life back to me, ready for the light of day.

I have been deeply shaped by living in this small Connecticut landscape with its stone walls, its brook, its hemlocks and maples, its small wild creatures. I want to know what has happened to me here in this garden place, what entered my being while I conducted my so-called ordinary life of eating, sleeping, earning a living, and paying my taxes. I want to experience my prints developing so that the images become clear to me, so that I know what has touched and formed me.

The farmhouse I live in sits on a little more than two acres. Once the farm itself was big. It had pastures, woodlots, hay fields, orchards, and gardens. Now a lawn and a stand of ash trees grow where the apple orchard once flourished. I know where it was because the gnarled dead trunks remain as evidence. At the back of the property there is a little pond. No doubt it was a drinking place for cattle. In the town records this is simply another suburban house lot, with a given number, on a given street.

But I have come to know that in these two acres there is intense and quiet activity that is *happening* twenty-four hours a day. I miss most of it. I get caught up in what must be done and therefore fail to experience the sunsets, the budding of the raspberries, the rusting of old farm implements in the earth, the building of wasp nests, and the death of old trees. But I feel the vibration of it all and I want to know this eventfulness better. Even just a little bit better!

To know in this way requires my presence and an openness to experience. I have to be willing to be intimate, to surrender my goal-setting, direction-oriented, controlling, self-defining self, in order to be encountered, to be met, to have a chance to be known. This is hard for me. The urge to be in control is so embedded in my body, my education, my culture, I feel helpless under its illusion.

That control and intimacy are mutually exclusive I know. Intimacy cannot be commanded or planned. It is not willed but happens by grace and opens the inner doors of the heart. It more readily happens when I lay no claim to anything and discover instead what is already present, already given.

All true intimacies are gifts. They appear as if from behind us, beside us, above us, below us. We usually cannot see them coming. They take our whole attention, and in the process we have a chance to come face-to-face with something we did not know about ourselves and the world.

To commune, to discover and to be discovered is deeply human. Real convergences are revelations that lift us out of ourselves, out of recoiling from any aspect of reality. We experience the Self then—all possessive pronouns gone—the joy of existence, which is the light within everything, the light that burns for its own sake declaring, "I am that I am." In that light, death, too, is experienced as a central part of life.

The Latin word for intimate is *intimus,* "inmost." I know that when I live in an "inmost" manner here in this old farm lot I see and know much more about the world and myself. I come to experience that each thing that dwells here with me is a saint of sorts. These are the presences, the events and experiences —the "inner photos"—I want to develop. To re- member, to hold, and to venerate the life around me, which sustains me, is a way to honor my personal mother. It is also a way to celebrate our common mother, the earth—the first and primary intimacy from which all other intimacy develops.

I hope as you read that you will think of the saints of the place where you live, whether that be a city street or a forest. The saints are all equal. They ask us to participate, to be fully here on earth. The fulcrum of this universe may ultimately be a passionate mutuality in which we surrender any separate definition of ourselves and discover that we are who we are together—in fundamental communion—in relationship with everything that is.

Newtown, Connecticut
November 1992

FALL

Leaves

T here are so many of them. Piles of them. I take pleasure in their abundance. More saints than you could ever dream of. Each one singular. Each one itself. Yellow, red, orange, parchment. They sail down in the autumn air like fearless sky divers. They are so trusting—letting go completely. Not questioning as I do . . . Will it be safe? Will I understand? Will it hurt? . . . stalling, qualifying, questioning, instead of releasing and taking to the air.

In the order of things here on my road the ash trees shed first. Their boatlike leaves sail away un-dramatically and early. After that the big sugar maple begins. It stands in perfect glory for about a week.

Then one windless night I sense that it sighs deeply somewhere inside its gnarled trunk and says, "Enough." The next day I see a waterfall of leaves. They fall, no, cascade down, rustling, pouring, to pool upon the ground like a large, golden puddle. Yellow earth-light illumines my face.

I have felt that glow before. On her last night my mother was aglow like that. She was radiant. Neither of us knew it was her last night. Standing in the kitchen she blazed like the maple tree and I said to her, "Mother, you are so beautiful." She smiled and nodded. "I have the glory in me," she said. Then quietly during the night, something in her declared, "Enough," and she shed her body. She let go. It was utterly clean. Only light remained.

Messy as the autumn leaves are in the yard, their process is clean. When the time comes to let go, they let go. With the help of my friend Keith, I take up the rake and we get the leaves to the compost pile. Heaps and heaps of leaves.

In grieving also, the affairs of the deceased must be gathered and gone through. The body is buried, and the composting of memory begins—the mystery of the years, layers and layers of shared life turning to soil in one's being.

I can feel it in myself. It is like a slow and constant heat. In this process I am aware that I can-not know what is happening until months later, sometimes years later. As in the decomposition of leaves, the *matter* of it all begins to alter. Memory shifts without my knowing about it. The very substance changes. Insights emerge. My own aging, like the weather, adds its part to this as does the living of every moment. As the heat continues the old breaks down and I experience something new emerging.

In my compost pile on the hill the leaves are of all different kinds. There are grass clippings too, weeds, small twigs, and kitchen leavings. As I turn the pile over everything joins with everything else. It is hard to know any longer what is what because it is mixed together, on the way to becoming one thing, soil. I take comfort in this. Through the seasons my memories are composted, too, and like the leaves they come together. Turned over and over, in time they finally turn into something new—rich, dark earth in the palm of my hand.

The Feral Cat

I have seen him now for seven years. These are
only glimpses—maybe two or three in the course
of many months. I sense him more than I see him . . .
a somewhat savage shadow that moves. His fur is the
color of underbrush, thick and matted. He could be
mistaken for a raccoon except when he turns his face
toward me and looks. Then I can see that he is a feral
cat, and very fine. I like knowing that he hunts and
survives on this property.

Him is how I think of the cat. All my instincts
tell me he should have no name, for his power lies in
the fact that he is wild and is determined to be so. I
think of him as a homeless one and I would wish him

whatever comfort there can be. Of course, as I think this, he lies under the lattices of the porch next to the warm foundation behind which the furnace churns and chugs.

If I happen to cross his path in the morning he hurries under the boxwood with a haughty turn of his head. I feel as if I have stepped on his private domain. And, of course, I have. He moved in here before I did.

My best look at him came one sunny day in mid-November. He had found a bank of leaves where sun would continue to shine for many hours. Snuggled down in brown brush and russet leaves, he disappeared except for the tufts of his ears. He knew I had seen him, and there was a challenge in his eyes. A feral saint. I couldn't take my eyes off him and he knew it.

We sat this way, he in the leaves and I in my chair, with the windowpane between us. The sun beat down. The minutes passed and then the hour. I felt akin to him and could feel myself becoming cat-like there in the leaves.

I could smell the wet, cold ground somehow, and the slightly dusty odor of leaves. I could feel warmth coming into me, reaching past fur to the bones, white precise bones. I could hear the rustle of a starling. Not worth hunting. Not worth moving my thawing body for. I could feel the rightness of this

7

bank, this place where no one owed me anything and I was free to be myself, free to care for myself. Hunt when hungry. Rest when tired.

I knew all the places to go. Under the lattice, into the leaf pile, close to the brush heaps in the woods to wait for grouse or chipmunk. I knew where the water was. I knew where to be when. This is not any kind of special time telling. Noon and sun are the same thing. Shade and hiding, one. Lunch and rabbit, a perfect unity. Something in me knew when to move and when to be still . . . my own nature . . . taking in the warmth, being here, homelessly at home.

I could see myself through the cat's eyes. I could sense his thinking, . . . "That one behind the glass . . . she's such a pale thing . . . no wildness in her. Safe and limited. Groomed. Careful. Predictable. Let her look. Let her see the other choice. Let her remember her own fur."

No address. No name. Ugly. Wild. Sensible. Living with no trace. Feral . . . free!

Mice

---

*B*y Thanksgiving the herb and vegetable gardens are all cleaned up. Dry stalks of tomato plants and twiggy stems of rosemary have been pulled from the ground. The yellow snarl of frozen nasturtium and the upright, black spotted remains of basil have been removed. Now I can see the small holes of animals in the ground, underground passageways and winter mansions of chipmunks and mice. Unbeknownst to me there has been careful construction under the canopy of late summer leaves.

Convenient food supplies are tucked away, and strategic entries made into the old cellar of the farmhouse. I know, because at this time of year I hear

9

cautious scurrying at night. The mice are taking up their winter life.

There is no way to keep them out of this house and garden. I have to share the place. The truth is that we live side by side, an intimate arrangement. There is only one of me, and many of them.

One year all my grass seed was consumed. I had carefully put it in a metal container in the garage, but by spring it was nothing but chaff. So, too, the bird-seed. The first year I lived with this, I felt frantic. Was my place infested? Were the mice chewing the electrical wires? Would I have to keep everything in metal tins? I put out traps. By the time the new growing season came there were still mice in the cellar. I considered poison. What to do?

I did not want to go on a killing rampage. I did not want to let the situation get out of hand. I never solved this quandary, but my attitude changed. It happened in the spring when I inadvertently found a mouse nest on a shelf in the garage. The nest was in, and also made of, an old mattress cover I used as a painting dropcloth. Curled up, surrounded by shredded fabric and cotton batting, were six baby mice . . . blind, hairless, and oh so vulnerable. I could see their hearts beating right through the skin. Their little chests heaved with each breath. They were a pink pulsing so sheer it could be snuffed out in an instant.

They must have been born only hours before. Could they sense their danger? Was the mother watching? Questions rose in me as fast as my awe at the vulnerability of these newborns. To be born is to be utterly exposed. I remember the sheer newness of my own two children when they were first born.

Then it struck me that each time I come into newness I, too, am pink like this, pulsing, and vulnerable. It has happened many times in my life, not just on day one. New relationships, new dwellings, new jobs, new understandings. My eyes do not quite function. My skin is paper thin. It is always a sheer time, an intimate time, when, like all newborns, I need protection badly.

So, of course, I left the nest just where it was, and some of my intolerant attitude also. Two weeks later the baby mice were gone. They were functioning. They were in the field, being field mice, not house mice. I shook out the dropcloth and thought about the *able* part of the word *vulnerable*. Able to sustain injury is what vulnerable means. Right!

Mice, who seem so skittery and afraid, are actually a brave lot. They have given me a new definition of brave—to feel the fear one has and to own it. Those who deny their fear are not brave.

By now I have looked a few mice directly in the eye. Encountered this way, they bristle out their whiskers like antennae. Their tiny black button eyes are unquestioning and steady. My admiration has grown with each of these exchanges.

The mice come and go. I come and go. When I am having Thanksgiving turkey, they are having seeds. So far they have not taken over the house. They are actually a modest few, for the local cat and the big black snake keep the population under control. Now when I hear rustling under the sink I am more willing to share . . . I have to, in any case. It is the nibbling saints, in autumn mode, sharing my house. And I *do* give thanks.

Bulldog

_S_trictly speaking Putnam does not reside in my garden. He lives catty-corner down the road. Still and all, I feel Putnam lives here, too, for he is in my yard often enough. His body, only six inches off the ground, wags its way into the driveway. His coat is an auburn, almost red color and ripples around him. Putnam is a very fat English bulldog of some advanced years.

His face looks as if he had pressed it up against the shop window of a dog delicatessen for weeks on end. I think his customary drool comes from gazing at those juicy bones displayed in a charcuterie for bull-dogs just like him. He lifts his face toward me with the innocence of a child and waits for me to love him.

Of course, I stop everything and give Putnam the attention his unselfconscious and enthusiastic presence seems to require. There is something natural, nonchalant, and humorous about his behavior. I smile and pet Putnam, and feel something else as well, something uncomfortable. When I look deeper into this discomfort I know I am embarrassed by Putnam.

His delight is obvious and flagrant. He turns over and presents his roly-poly stomach for stroking. "Put your hand right there. Good! A little higher, please." Wiggle, wiggle, the sausage body moves along the loose stones of the driveway positioning itself to get the perfect sensation. There seems to be no pride in the dog, just direct, unadulterated pleasure seeking . . . hence the name my daughter-in-law and I have given him privately . . . Putnam, the Pleasure Pig.

I wonder how different life would be for me if I could be as lacking in self-doubt and self-judgment as Putnam. His whole being demonstrates an assumption that he is a lovable creature, a deserving creature, and an enjoyable one. His fat, aged self simply squirms with the sacred knowledge that he is one of God's creatures. Such direct light makes me turn my eyes away.

To act as if one had the total endorsement of the

universe behind one's particular existence would be extraordinary! I hedge my bets by offering to others what I myself want, by restricting my requests for love and help to those I know will not reject me out of hand. I am oh, so careful, whereas I could, with a Putnam-like trust, meet the world with a joyful, natural wag.

I study Putnam and try to unlearn my embarrassment. Someone told me once that embarrassment was misplaced radiance. What is rightly placed radiance? It must have something to do with the glowing ease of being what one is, and feeling the endorsement of belonging to life itself.

I observe Putnam's ease. He lies in the middle of the road where the sun shines and warms the tarmac. If he must, he moves for cars. Mostly cars move for him. And if it should happen that his desirous, loving nature does not meet with appropriate affection, he walks off with a "too-bad-for-them" attitude. Not daunted or belittled in the slightest, he seeks his own counsel and pleasure under the mailbox. Neither will Putnam reject because he was rejected. He will be open to pleasure again . . . meeting a stranger or an old acquaintance with renewed interest in the possibilities of exchange. No smoldering grudges here or careful tallies of past slights.

Putnam is not, in fact, trying to attain something. He is simply meeting the world with his pleasure-nature, inviting those who can to join his radiance . . . light with light. I want to participate in this direct and happy warmth. I want to let my love and pleasure out so it can meet the love and pleasure of others directly.

WINTER

White Ash

I t's late December. The leaves have all fallen and the trees stand naked. Stripped, the trees have a sculptured look, and I have the curious sensation that I can both see and hear better in these winter woods. The wind is blowing hard. Above my head, tree limbs are clashing, making boisterous, wooden music. Here below, where I stand, the trunks seem to glow. On their bark the lichen shimmers in the blue-gray light of this season. Subtle, muted colors . . . ochre, gray-white and the palest moss green . . . patinas made by slow quiet growth.

This is the stuff of life and of art. Nothing dramatic . . . just years of persistence . . . growing in the same place . . . extending a little farther . . . becoming a little more. A quiet work that enlarges by seasons. I think of my mother, whose art grew quietly, persistently throughout her whole life.

What is homely and seemingly inconsequential becomes important in winter. In this woodlot of stripped ash trees and brush, one little bush shines with red berries. The berries seem to shout with color. "We are here," they call to the birds. "Eat us, digest us, spread our seeds so we can multiply." This is interrelatedness with a purpose.

But the berries do something else as well with no obvious purpose. Their color, in this otherwise brown and green canvas, makes it possible to see everything more clearly. Twenty red berries in an acre of brown. The stripped trees make the berries visible. The berries make the ash trees visible. They reveal and reflect one another and yet remain independent. Together they are more without losing themselves. In winter light this is so visible to me. It is pure interplay. I want my human relationships to have this intimacy, this ease.

Bare bones of ash trees . . . shimmering berries . . . lichen growing without ambition, just true to its lichen nature. When I allow myself to be and allow others to be just as they are, what wonderful bare bones of connection that is. When I can notice and savor the many flashes of color that happen in life, the bright berries of delight, what constant praise that is. When I can be patient and know that what develops over time . . . little by little . . . with consistency . . . is what ultimately is rewarded and lasts, what wonderful relaxation in growth that is. I can stop hurrying to be what I cannot yet be, and rest simply in what I am now.

Above me the leafless crowns of the ash trees move against each other. The sound is that of wooden tongues speaking or singing a foreign language with glottal stops. I do not understand a word, but I feel the music. Something happens in my belly when I hear it. Somehow I am singing, too, and being sung . . . it is a different kind of understanding. Fifteen feet above my head a grand, important orchestra is playing the winter chorale of the white ashes.

Wooden voices singing a capella in the chill wind. I listen and feel the wordless branches in myself, joining the allegro. It is winter solstice time. The dark turns again to light. I feel called to praise. Oh, sing the turning of the year. Sing the season. Sing with whatever can sing. Clap hands and branches. Let all that has life be glad. More understanding than my life can wish for is this urge to praise. Rejoice and again rejoice!

Tracks on New Snow

December thirty-first. The new calendar year will start tomorrow. I am aware that it is a year my mother will not share. My breath catches and I go outside.

New snow has fallen. That helps. Like a white sheet of beautiful paper, the snow is a parchment ready for writing. I will read many things on this paper. It will inform me.

My friend Jack, a longtime observer of nature, says that he can feel the presence and mystery of a creature almost more strongly in its tracks than in its appearance. One can study life-as-lived in animal tracks, life-as-process, the marks of what has been and still is, somehow simultaneously together.

One can dream oneself into those blue-black shadows in the snow and sense the motivation of another creature. I am sure that in the white snow cover of our minds our intentions are marking dark tracks all the time. I know there are beaten paths, entrenched habits, that keep me from exploring new ground. I am not aware of those trails and how deeply they have been laid down in me. I do not even know the self who treads upon them.

To study motivation is to study one's own tracks. Is there time to catch that movement which is before movement? The movement, like an animal's instinct, prior to thought, and alive in the very cells themselves? That movement which forms thought, which is the substance and event of thought? This is where those old predators, fear and desire, can be faced. This is the place where true self-expression will be discovered, if it ever can be.

In the fine white snow of this December day I see how a rabbit came this way into brushy piles by the stone wall. Was it escaping . . . running in fear? Was it foraging . . . trying to feed the constant desire of its stomach? Was it leaping for the sheer joy of movement? Rabbit tracks . . . I dream myself into the vulnerable creature that made them . . . so much like me. Heart pounding a mile a minute, often stopped and frozen in fear, or scurrying for cover.

This white snow is like an empty mind. It is beautiful. Without tracks it is beautiful. With tracks it is beautiful. I can learn here. I can discover experiences occurring, moment by moment, like small explosions . . . the "big bangs," albeit in miniature, of this constantly becoming world.

I follow the rabbit's path. The back paws leave bigger shadows. There is something even, rhythmic, in the spaces between front paws and back, in the repeating of their pattern. I follow, and leave my own pattern in the new snow.

One time last winter I saw some tracks stop: Hip hop . . . hip hop . . . hip hop . . . and then complete stop. Unbroken snow. No evidence of violence. No explanation. No continuation. No tracks anywhere. Nothing but white snow.

Was the rabbit transmuted? A transfigured saint? An "Assumption"? I don't know. It is a mystery. I smile to feel again how life-giving the unsolvable is. I want to live with mystery . . . bounding into the heart of the world, into the new snow of this moment and the new year.

Thaw

February. The days are getting lighter. I feel relief. The sun, for the past two weeks or more, is
warmer. I can hear the water running in the brook,
which was dry only a few weeks back. Everything is
trickling. Little rivulets of water move in the grass,
among tree roots, under the leaves. Walking out in
the woods I find that my shoes stick in the soft
ground. As I raise my boot, the earth makes a slurpy,
muddy sound, as of juicy, exaggerated kissing.

Sm-a-a-a-ck! This sound makes me smile. The
soles of my feet are happy. I am enjoying this. It's February and close to Valentine's Day. I am celebrating wet
earth. I am celebrating a break in the below-twenty

degrees that has been so relentless for the past weeks. February thaw . . . messy and wonderful. I can almost sniff spring, though it is not an odor that can actually be smelled.

This is the time to see what winter damage has happened in the garden. It is the time to pore over seed catalogs, and to keep my gardener's greed in check. Living alone, I know I am limited in what I can do . . . just so much! I have to be willing to look at the glossy catalogs and say, "NO."

In this mild winter weather everything appears hopeful and possible. A little more sun and the garden looks as if it is already blooming—weed-free and glorious. This is an image I have learned not to trust, for by late June, with too much to take care of, the pleasure of this garden turns into a chore. Then I grumble. I resent everything to do with maintenance. I have no leisure and hence no delight.

Leisure and delight . . . they are wedded. Without leisure there is no time to feel and to savor. Their rhythm allows things to grow at an organic pace. If I can really match that pace I will recall that the "inmost" garden of the world is fundamentally leisurely. Vegetation has its seasons. The moon has its month. The sun has its day. The universe is orderly and is always on time.

I look at the seed catalogs and from them I get an artificial sense that anything and everything can be grown. With effort and at a price! If I forced flowers, started seeds, bought artificial light, I could have something splendid even now in the winter gloom. But this I have painfully learned is not for me. Having lost my leisure over and over again, I must be abstinent now in order to have what I really need . . . time to feel and to be in the place I live. It's February and that means it is winter still, a time when I can be spare and love it.

Spare . . . knowing that less is more. Less need to improve, less trying, less judgment, less regret. I am learning about this, year after year. Slowly the self-imposed abstinence gives me freedom. This is not always an easy process. It often feels like dying. Perhaps I am practicing for the day when I will have to give up everything, when I will be in another garden altogether.

To say "no" to hurry, to overwork, to whatever is more than is needed, is to say "yes" to leisure, to reverie, to communion. It is a "dying-to-live" process. I want this to be my February thaw.

Out into this mild, winter weather I go to reconnoiter and to pick up small sticks for kindling. I cannot do anything about the garden now. This is the season when the garden is truly and simply lying fallow. And I must follow suit. In that state, restoration goes on in ways that are not apparent and are yet essential. For me that means going out into the world of snow puddles and melting icicles instead of ordering seeds. It means experiencing the land without a plan for it.

As I walk in the woodlot my shoes make a squashy sound. Suddenly something moves near the brush piles. A loud bounding. Then I see the white flag of a deer make a few graceful arcs up over the nearby ridge and out of sight. My heart pounds a little with the surprise.

I notice now that I am suddenly alert, that I have exchanged any notion of efficiency for the experience of attentiveness. With the movement of another creature I have remembered my creatureliness. I feel a confirmation in this. I am in ever present time now, God's time, alive time.

I can feel the melting world—everything wet and waiting. The leaves, matted down since they first fell, can be picked up in sheets, almost like filo dough. Deep down the ground is still frozen. February . . . full of spring, and full of cold that is yet to come.

I listen to the brook water running in the culvert and down into my neighbor's yard. It moves along at a happy, burbling pace, flowing with a steady volume. It stays within its banks. It follows the path of least resistance and is yet consistent with itself. Trickling, gurgling, bubbling . . . on it goes . . . not missing any ground it travels over . . . filling up the hollow spaces . . . moving on . . . moving on. I want to garden and to live this way. Staying within my capacity. Filling the space. Enjoying each season. Planting, cultivating, pruning, harvesting, lying fallow. Moving on in God's time, leisure time . . . thawing into spring.

Geese

Some distance to the east and north of me are two large airports. When I am outside I can hear the droning of the planes in their flying pattern over this section of the county. The silver bodies glint above the tips of the ash trees. Their white contrails leave patterns in the sky. These 747s have been places, and in the brief moment they fly above this small suburban plot I feel a sympathetic nudge from the faraway. Every year I have flown to Europe to see my mother. No need this year. Everything seems to remind me of that. No need. Not this year.

Geese come flying over, too. They land at their own local airports . . . two large bodies of water to the southeast and west of me. Much of the water supply for the county is drawn from these reservoirs. Most of the geese winter here, but some have been to other continents, filling their feathers with heat and tropical air. It's early March and they have returned. I like knowing where they have been, especially in this cold snap.

Sometimes there are only a few birds flying in formation. Sometimes there are twenty or more. I get a rush of hopeful feeling when I hear them honking. I have never completely understood why. At first I thought it was because they had the freedom of the skyways . . . something high and romantic . . . something in contrast to my earthbound existence. But lately I have learned more about geese through an article a friend brought to share. This new information has fleshed out that spontaneous inner feeling of mine.

What I learned is that of all the creatures that I can see in this landscape, the geese best represent the communion of saints. They depend on one another. The lead goose does the most work, but when it is tired, it falls back and another takes its place. To be able to rely on others is a deep trust that does not come easily.

The geese fly in the wake of one another's wings. They literally get a lift from one another. I want to be with others this way. Geese tell me that it is, indeed, possible to fly with equals.

The high honking I hear when I stand on the ground and look up is the sound of encouragement the geese make to keep on flying. It is a loud and happy sound in my ears. I want to honk with others on the journey.

The geese fly over, signaling what it is to be in communion and community. My heart feels glad. The old victory sign was a **V**. The geese make this sign as they fly by. And I do the same with my fingers raised high in snappy salute.

SPRING

Peepers

I listen for them now. They are to me the first sound of spring. In the early mornings their high trill begins to rise from the cattle pond and the nearby marsh. A life sign.

I have never laid eyes on them. But as spring advances their chorus grows until there is a continuous high pitch day and night. "The waters are warm enough. The sun is warm enough. Live," they sing. "Come forward. Live."

In old Scandinavian lore fires are burned on the last day of April. These fires are meant to melt Old Man Winter down to the ground. Young folk jump over the embers. Couples make love.

People drink and dance and embrace the new season.

Just before May Day last year my siblings and I took our mother's ashes and buried them. Rain fell in sheets that April day. It was bleak. Although yellow tulips could be bought in the florist shops there was a bitter chill in the air. We were frozen to the core. The awesomeness of placing the urn with our mother's remains down in the stony vault next to our father's urn was bone sobering. These were only the ashes. Not our parents. We said this to one another and gazed further back into the vault where the urns of those before them stood solemnly. Grandmother. Grandfather.

We said the words of passage, and tried to sing in our wavering voices the hymns we had picked. We sounded very feeble and off-key in the rain, in the cold, in the bleak truth that our parents were gone. I think we buried a little of ourselves there. And we took with us the certain knowledge that we are the generation now living, the one on which our children lean.

As we rode back from the cemetery the minibus was full of silence. Only the monotonous flip-flop of the windshield wipers counted off the kilometers. From time to time, between cloudbursts, we had glimpses of the countryside. There we could see the fields dotted with big brush piles. Prunings, windfall, and building scraps, gathered for almost a year, lay ready for the torch on Walpurgis Night, the night when the cold is burned to the ground.

These rituals help. Smelling the smoke the night following the burial we could cry a little more easily. I know now that I am mourning my mother through every season of the year. We all mourn this way. The first Christmas without the beloved, the first New Year. We will feel the loved one not here for the first bloom of forsythia, not here for the ripening of the pears, not here . . . not here. . . .

The peepers are wailing. How is it that one feels loss so much more deeply in spring than at any other time? Loss moves like a drill through my body, like the high-pitched voices of these young frogs. But they are singing a new song. "The sun is warm enough. The waters are warm enough. Live. Come on. Live!"

Saints Shrill. Hundreds of them. Could it be that by sheer dint of their noisy insistence the last of Old Man Winter melts into water and runs off, taking a portion of grief along in the bargain?

Skunk Cabbage

S kunk cabbages begin to poke their leaves out of the mud. In the low-lying parts of the woodlot their hefty leaves push and prod forward into spring. They are the free-form sculptures of these woods. You either like them or hate them. They grow in profusion. I had better like them, it seems.

It is early April now. The mosquitoes have laid their larvae on the stagnant water between the dark green leaves of the skunk cabbages. Birds call. Buds are knobbing up on the trees and bushes. I feel an ache in the air ... the swollen ache of life pushing forward, bursting its seams.

Determined to watch the cabbages grow, I have

been going out to inspect their progression. The upward surge of the leaves is astounding. You can almost hear them growing, sopping up moisture. They gain an inch a day, it seems. This is cabbage intelligence. They must do this while it's wet enough. They must do this while the canopy of the trees is not shutting the light out for their initial growth.

I think how something in me wants to grow, too, when the opportunity is at hand. There is an urgency . . . an "it-won't-wait" feeling. But to really experience this, and to act on it, is not so easy. It means listening.

I practice with the cabbages. I listen to them. Are they humming? Buzzing? I sense a vibration without sound that is yet a sound. I hear/feel it. Can I learn to hear/feel the same in me? I think this is the sound the Bible speaks of . . . "In the beginning was the Word." In the beginning was the Word, meaning the Vibration, I believe. All that exists has been sounded. I think we are configured through this noiseless vibration which is movement and being all at once. We are named by it, oscillated, electromagnetically uttered into life.

To listen, then, to the name we are given to be, is a profound act of resonance. I think Saint Cabbage does it sitting there . . . squat and green . . . firmly planted in the sump of the woods. It obeys its given nature. I want to be as secure in mine, to feel the vibration that is naming me from the soles of my feet to the roots of my hair. And since a part of that naming is to bear my drawbacks, I ask to learn to stink as the cabbages do, directly. No psychic deodorant. No cover-up. I want to believe that these stocky, green skunks of the woods are giving me, their two-legged friend, a hearty encouragement from deep within the muck and ooze of spring and the vernal equinox.

Wildflowers

---

*T*he leaves are out. They are a sheer light green, and I am surprised by their shadows. Now I see patterns on the ground again, patches of dark and light. My feet walk a dappled path.

A sweet smell wafts toward the house from the woods. When I first smelled it, I thought a very special plant must be the source. It took a while to determine that this scent was Essence of Eastern Woods, a combination of organic matter, young ferns, and wildflowers. Over the years I have waited for that odor. A quiet smell that is utterly intimate. It opens me.

This is the time to hunt for Dutchman's

breeches, patches of green with a hovering cloud of white pantaloonlike flowers. Now is the time to find the light pink of wild geranium, and the deep magenta of trilliums hidden under their trefoil leaves. Solomon's seal is out. The ferns are uncurling. Jack is preaching in his pulpit. Indian pipe and lady's slipper, those protected species, are also emerging. They are all there in their appointed places, shy woodland saints. I love finding them again and again, predictable and wild, elusive and perennial. The woods fill with their sweetness.

In spiritual texts there is mention of perfumed states of mind. In deep concentration odors can be perceived so honeylike that one is called to remember the beauty of the soul. Maybe that is why we are drawn to very specific fragrances, fragrances that remind us of our deepest being. And is not smell the most intimate of the senses? We inhale odor, we take it deeply into us.

The wildflower saints provoke me to remember the steadiness of return, year after year. They tell me that one does not need to be cultivated to be beautiful. They tell me that the soul remembers its essence, if it is given room to grow. I bow to the shy trillium, the wild geranium, the jack-in-the-pulpit, the lady's slipper, the Dutchman's breeches, the Indian pipes, the ferns, Solomon's seal, and the columbine.

These gentle flowers remind me that we surrender to no one finally but to our own soul, to the essence of ourselves, which is hidden in God. Sweet and wild is the experience of surrender. There is nothing more intimate.

Purple Finches

A pair of purple finches begins to circle the house in late April. This is their territory. They look for a likely spot and begin gathering twigs, bits of string, pine needles, and other nest-building materials. He is rosy and large. She is mostly gray, and smaller.

The two are now old friends of mine. I like to guess where they'll put their nests this time. They build two . . . a false one as a decoy and the real one. Mrs. Finch even sits in the decoy nest to fool the predatory world.

One year the real nest was built in the decorative wreath on the front door. I could not believe my good fortune in being able to watch their nesting ingenuity from indoors. Unfortunately someone else was watching, too. Four eggs of a lovely blue-green color were laid. When the eggs were almost ready to hatch the nest was raided by the neighbor's black cat. I was heartbroken.

The finches came back the following year and built a nest on the porch light fixture . . . a little higher than the cat could reach. But from then on I knew that their real nest was hidden high in the hemlock while the decoys were easy to see somewhere on available ledges around the house.

I have noticed this decoy maneuver in myself also. I will often look very busy about something entirely different to keep safe the brooding and hatching of something precious. I build a decoy activity, so to speak, for I know that too much light, or outside interest, directed toward a creative inner process pillages the nest. Nothing can hatch.

To incubate a book, a poem, a drawing, an idea, or a new attitude, I need an inner nest. The twigs of association must be gathered. The materials to make a safe place for incubation must be quietly put together. If this process is disturbed a whole new nest must be built. I have to start over. But I cannot start over too many times. There is not enough psychic strength.

For myself the secret of secrecy is to tell *all* to

someone I love and trust, if the secret is about pain or shame of any kind. But if the secret is about an inner process that needs time to develop, then I must wait until the pregnancy is far enough along to bear exposure.

Turtles cover their eggs. Finches build decoy nests. Mothers grow silently large with child. We have an instinct to surround the new with time, with protection, with secrecy. I am grateful for the ways this has been done for me.

I have yet to see any baby finches. My purple pair do a good job of protecting their brood. I feel good about their skill in this. New creatures are born for their own sake, for their own lives, not for the benefit of parents or curious bystanders. Like books, like paintings, like poems. . . .

I am simply grateful that Mr. and Mrs. Finch find this garden good enough to raise a family in. May the little saints fly in their own time.

Dahlias

I go down into the cellar and find dahlia tubers from the fall. They are wizened ugly things. I can hardly believe these brown and wrinkled lumps of matter are going to be flowers in less than two months.

It is early May now and the ground is warming up. Even if we should have one more frost these tubers will be safe in the ground. I have tried to sort out their colors so that I will have mostly white and yellow flowers. Right now the tubers all look the same and I have a kind of color roulette on my hands. By the end of June there may be a bank of yellow and white dahlias punctuated by a solitary, flaming red one. A surprise. A red flag. So be it!

I feel glad to be in my shirtsleeves, trowel in hand. The west side of the house has a stone wall close to its foundation. A bed has been dug there, and that is where the dahlias are going.

These are the small variety and do not have to be set very deeply in the ground. I spade up the dirt and put one of the tubers in. By fall this one will have produced several more, not unlike potatoes. I just have to wait.

This is easy gardening. I like it, and yet I am a little suspicious about easy things. Pop the tuber in and forget it. If the weather is dry, add water. It's a foolproof recipe. I feel a little ashamed when I get compliments on any of my fast and easy recipes . . . it seems the results shouldn't be that good with so little effort.

This, of course, is Northern European conditioning. Hard is good. Easy is soft and suspicious. These private or cultural evaluations have nothing to do with how things fundamentally are. The intrinsic way must be the easiest way, and I want to learn to trust that now. Standing by the stone wall I ask myself: "What is doing the growing around here?" I answer: "Something in the dahlias themselves. I am simply present to enjoy this."

I spade up a place in the bank for each tuber. In

they go! I replace the earth. I do not have to do anything more. I do not have to sweat. The dahlias know what to do. Leaves will come. Flowers will come. Some years they will even be profuse. Then the dahlias will die. I will dig up the tubers. I will put them in the cellar. And they will be planted again the following year if all things remain the same. Which is as likely to be true as not to be true.

Can I live this dahlia way, too? A way that does not complicate, does not avoid, or force things to happen? A direct way that simply opens . . . allowing for process? To plant, to flower in the sun, and to surrender to frost when it comes, this way is thorough. It occurs in every aspect of life and skips nothing. It is living and dying, again and again. It is so simple, this allowing, and so profound. I read in the dictionary that the root meaning of the word *suffer* is *allow*. This stirs me.

In the pale May sunshine, with a tuber in each hand, I ask: What is easy? What is hard? I don't know. They are all mixed up now in my mind. But I do know that these tubers, wizened root balls, are full of summer color . . . full of allowing. Saint Dahlia. As I tuck you into soil, I want to trust that I am tucked in, too, embedded in that matrix which supports all form. Then whatever color is within me will emerge with little effort.

Poison Ivy

*M*ay. The poison ivy leaves are beginning to come out on the vines. They are slightly copper-colored and oily. Poison ivy grows happily in this county of Connecticut. In fact, it is the most luxuriant crop on this property. By June its leaves will be glossy and green. If they did not cause such a skin disturbance they would be a most popular ground cover.

I have learned to respect the plant and watch out for it. A cake of yellow soap is always at hand by the kitchen sink in case I inadvertently brush up against these leaves. Some people handle their poison with poison. They spray, year after year, and eventually some parts of their gardens are free of the vines. I do not feel comfortable with this method for I do not know what other effects I will be causing.

I do not feel comfortable doing nothing either. John, my son, put copper nails in the thick hairy vines growing up the trunks of maple and ash. Some of the vines he severed. But this has very little effect on their profusion.

I notice that wherever there is a great deal of poison ivy, there is also a bounty of jewelweed. They are companion plants. From jewelweed a very fine itching salve can be made. Things are often paired up like this in nature. They balance each other and form a whole of some sort.

This happens in the internal ecology, too. I see in myself how an extreme of any kind always constellates the opposite. If I fall into work addiction my body will sooner or later give out and I will have to experience doing absolutely nothing for a period of time. If I pride myself on being a thoughtful and consistently courteous person, I am sure to turn unexpectedly vicious.

The poison will form and will surely find its way to expression. An antidote is needed. I can see this balancing act very clearly in the consuming of foods. If I eat too much sugar I want something salty to go with it. If I use a heavy stimulant I want something bland to soothe my nervous system.

Poison ivy and jewelweed. Over time it is never just one or the other. How often have I thought I was absolutely right about something, and in being adamant I lost the fabric of relatedness and the situation became all wrong. I keep forgetting that events arise in relationship to each other. They grow simultaneously. They are neither this nor that . . . and yet they occur because of this and that. They make each other happen.

Something that looks like poison may lead to something very good. Something seemingly wonderful can have the seeds of destruction in it. I have no way of being sure . . . the living of that tension is so very hard. I will always be right and wrong. Safe and in danger. Strong and weak. Loving and uncaring. Stupid and smart. Aware and unconscious.

I know this as I walk here in the woodlot and despair over the profusion of green and glossy leaves. Too much to ever be rid of! These leaves are here for good, like the ivy inside me. I take comfort in the stately stands of jewelweed that grow here as well— tall, tumescent, with lovely little orange flowers. May they be inside me, too.

With the poison is the jewel, and vice versa. Ivy and weed. Two kinds of saints. They are my teachers. I hold them in mind, and a bar of yellow soap in hand.

The Quince Tree

I have wondered if my old quince tree dates back as far as the original structure of the farmhouse, 1840? The quince is in bloom now. Its little white flowers are such a contrast to its dark brown trunk. They shine and are completely new while the tree itself looks ancient. Twisted and gnarled, it appears to me like an aged, modern dancer, whose every limb is going off in some contorted, asymmetrical direction. Here and there bark has peeled off in long strips, to hang like a skimpy dance costume around the exposed trunk.

Every year I think that this will be the last year for the old tree. And then here it is again . . . in bloom. By late August its furry, pearlike fruit will be hanging there for the birds and for me. Some years there are only two or three quinces. Sometimes I gather as many as ten.

I respect this tree very much. It is the crone of the garden. And though it is, in fact, rather ugly, I would miss its presence very much should a winter wind take it down. Its dark shape in the middle of a very green lawn seems appropriate. A great-great-grandmother tree that is still bearing fruit.

I observe Mother's Day with this old tree. I cannot call my mother anymore. I miss that very much. I cannot call my grandmother. I am the grandmother now and I do not know how to really be that. Not yet, anyway. So I stand here in the garden and try to feel the old tree.

I want to learn from it. One thing I have understood is that I can bear fruit even into the later years of my life. I see that in the tree. It also tells me of the power of roots. This tree would not be standing now without some wonderful taproot holding it in place. I want to believe that I am growing a root like that into the ground of my being.

The tree tells me that new flowers are new flowers no matter what we look like, and that beauty comes in many forms.

There are other fruit trees here on the lawn. Two pears. One peach. Two plums. They are younger trees and they, too, are in bloom just now.

But the long-lived quince tree is different. It is a *presence* that seems to come forward to meet me. I find myself talking to the tree, addressing it with deference. "Old Grandmother," I say, "how are you this fine Mother's Day?" I swear the tree answers with a little groan, or a sigh. Not a complaint. It is an old tree talking.

"Nice flowers," I say.

"They'll do," mutters the tree. (Matter-of-fact tone that indicates there is no need to gild the lily.)

"Anything you want?" I continue.

"A little water would be nice. Just leave the hose running a few minutes. And don't fuss. That's the main thing. Don't fuss. Things are just fine the way they are. Remember that."

"I'll try to," I say. "But how do I know that they are just fine?"

"You don't until you find it out."

"Please explain, Old Grandmother."

"I will, but only this once. The more you worry the more worry you have. So don't fuss. Just do or don't do. That's all. Second-guessing wastes your life. I'm blooming and that's it. Enough."

"Yes, Grandmother," I say, and fetch the garden hose. But I don't leave it. I stand there and water. Just that. I do this. I water on this fine day in May. Mother's Day.

Turning Soil

Now spring is really here. Everything smells verdant and fresh. I am drawn outside to grub in the ground. It's the green time, the time to turn the soil in the vegetable garden.

Under the leaves of the compost lies new earth. I spade it up bit by bit and heap it up in the wheelbarrow. The soil smells of moisture and nutrients. I am enjoying how black it is . . . full of organic materials . . . full of potential.

Down the little hill I go with the weight of the blue wheelbarrow tugging at my arms. How to design this year's vegetable garden? Two hills for zucchinis, one row for sugar peas, one for beans, one for both

New Zealand spinach and chard to share, one for lettuce. Nooks and crannies for cucumbers, which can climb up and over the protective stone wall.

I spread the new earth on last year's rows. Grubbing in the ground. It feels wonderful. I've become a kid with permission to be dirty. I am getting more than exercise here. Earth-connected, soil-sprinkled, humus-spread, I am turning everything over.

The rows look handsome now, mounded up and ready. I feel hopeful. Expectant. It's preparation time when all is possible. Next to the trowel lies an assortment of seed packets and small flats of tomatoes, basil, and eggplants. The seeds are all different. Beans, sturdy and singular. They can be planted one at a time with precision. I can place each white, kidney-shaped seed. The lettuce seeds, on the other hand, are almost poured into place from the packet. A fine dark dusting is sprinkled down the row to be covered loosely with earth.

Depth of planting, time of planting, proximity of plants to one another. These are all considerations. Eggplants must be moved every year. Tomatoes like the same old place in the garden and flourish well with basil as the companion plant. Snow peas and lettuce like the cool of early summer. New Zealand spinach prefers the later, warmer part. Zucchini does well in slightly sandy soil as do the root crops. It's hard to keep track of all these preferences. But they make the difference between a fine yield and a mediocre one.

Each one of these seed varieties has its own nature, its own way in the garden. If I want a good crop I have to learn about this. My inner nature, too, has its organic leanings. To go against my self will harm my development. I must acknowledge this in me and in others. To really yield we must respect our own nature.

I poke holes to drop the seeds in. Covered by new soil, each in their own place, the seeds wait for sun, for rain, and for their life force to produce the first delicate showing of green. I love this mystery. Each day I will come here to witness it.

It's grubbing-in-the-ground time. Thoroughly dirty from it all, I sprinkle a little earth on myself for good measure. Why not? I am planted in this garden too.

Impatiens

All danger of frost over, the time has come to plant the impatiens. The property is very shady, and these annuals fill in and give color to the place. They like the conditions and do very well here.

I get many flats of them. For the most part they are the pink, salmon-colored variety. Occasionally I buy white ones as well. Into the tubs and beds they go. It is rather simple-minded ... an all-of-a-kind gardening.

For years I tried other things. I wanted variety and flamboyant color. Of course, the most riotous bloomers are plants that need sun. Since my yard is full of shade nothing much came of those experiments.

I had to submit to planting the one annual that does splendidly here—the humble impatiens.

I can feel my exasperation at being about to do the very same kind of flower planting again this year. My need for variety is thwarted by very real conditions. Impatiens plants need shade and they luxuriate here. With their small, four-petaled flowers they make the place beautiful. And their very profusion creates a special richness. Why do I resist the obvious? I plant the flats and try for some equanimity . . . while knowing there's an irony here . . . I am impatient with these impatiens.

This feeling is familiar. I have it every now and then when I meditate. Something within me resists repeating the same old thing—following the breath, keeping the mind focused, sitting still. I resist the repetition because in the very act of repetition I discover over and over again what the real conditions are within me . . . restlessness . . . need for reassurance . . . fear that life is passing me by and that I am missing something . . . the need for distraction, for entertainment. My mind tries to find ways around itself, resisting the truth. All the shaded parts of my awareness come to light as I sit still, as I repeat the practice over and over again.

The circumstances of this garden suit impatiens to a T. The circumstances of my life could suit me to a T, too, if I would allow myself just to be here. I could enjoy this one-of-a-kind gardening and feel its rightness.

I could simply enjoy living alone instead of questioning it, wondering if I am doing something wrong. I could find relaxation in conducting my work as a therapist . . . letting the hours of faithful attendance to others accumulate in meaning both for me and for them. Life could be simple, without effort. Easy. Why don't I garden and live in this direct way: take up the very same thing again and again and again, and slowly come through to the heart where all things flourish?

I don't have any answers. Resistance is so familiar. It keeps me from feeling the fear of surrendering to the obvious, the fluid way: just doing what needs doing, lending myself year after year to what can grow within me and around me. That means planting impatiens just now. But this acceptance of ease is frightening to me, for behind its apparent appeal lies a light-filled void. There a personality could truly disappear. Nothing to do. Nowhere to go. No one to be . . . the death of *me*. The beginning of spring.

Peonies

With a bundle of stakes under my arm and a green ball of twine in hand I go to the peony bed. It lies in full sun and is shaped like a crescent moon. I stand there and see how leggy the peonies have gotten. Their buds are hard and heavy. Already the plants are bending toward the ground. They need support and it is time to stake them.

For weeks I have been watching the peonies emerge. At first they are just a hint of red in the dark soil. Then more happens. Something round and head-like pushes upward into the world. It looks bloody. Like a birth. Not just one, but many, many births.

Not long after, solid red stems stand erect in the

moon-shaped bed. Their shapes are visible through the living room window even in the dark. I always think of them as a tribe of red people who have ascended from below—materialized their spirits to this place—tunneled up from some dream state or territory that has once given them life. Then they are here, eager to live in the new world.

We are born this way, too, emerging into this life from some other place, ready to live where we are planted. Ready to be at risk and think nothing of it. At least to begin with.

Now it is June. The solstice will soon be here. The peony leaves are growing dark green and glossy. There are fewer leaves on the plants this year and this gives the illusion that the plants are taller. I hide a stake in the middle of a peony clump, cut the twine, and gather the plants in my arms. A peony hug! The fingers of my two hands try to find each other while my face is deep in the leaves. I feel my way to making a knot. The circle of twine must close but not too tightly. A little tug to make sure that it will hold, and I let the plants go. They spring back and right themselves. They look braced, and I am aware that I have been embraced by peony leaves along my whole torso. A fair exchange.

"Peony hugging," I think to myself as I move from clump to clump. Each place I become more aware of the hard and heavy buds. Their weight has already begun to bend the stems toward the ground. In a few days the blossoms will open, and they will be huge. The whole plant will groan.

I think of human blossoming and how much it, too, needs to be staked and supported. We need a circle of friends to hold us if we are going to open like peony buds and let out the beauty that is in us.

How many of us have keeled over just in the time of blooming for lack of support and encouragement? How many of us have not dared to reveal our true selves because we fear being cut, we fear the dying afterward? How many of us say to life, "This is a mistake. I can't do it. It takes more than I've got"?

It does take everything we've got. I walk around the bed. It is a cradle. The plants reach my navel now. Some have only one bud. Some have two, and some have as many as six blossoms. Their peony natures have said "yes" and have opened. The petals radiate out—white with pink—pink with white. I want to find the nature in me that will say "yes" like this. And I want to support others in their blooming . . . to be a stake, a circle of twine, an encouragement, a witness.

SUMMER

The Pond

_A_ path leads through the underbrush, under the tall canopy of the mastlike ash trees. Summer has come. July, but I am no longer sure if it is this year, last year, or next year. It does not matter. The little pond is dark, a muddy color. I can see the leaves of many autumns in the bottom of it, russet, brown and gray. On its surface are water lilies. They float like dreams, lit by a yellow white light. From time to time a bubble rises from the murky bottom as if the roots wanted to share in the light too.

Much is always happening here. The spring peepers are not as noticeable now—the heavy plop at the far shore tells me the bullfrogs have reached maturity. From time to time a "glunk" rises like the sound of deep swallowing. And then the chorus starts—like sawing near the waterline.

A young maple leans out over the pond to create a leafy umbrella. Its shadow makes the water's surface reflect more purely. Sky and trees are drawn down here to the level of my feet, yet they are also above me. A dragonfly—electric blue with black wings—lands on a witch hazel leaf next to my thigh. An ancient insect, its color is startling—a shock of iridescent brightness in the shade upon shade of apple green, hunter green, blue green under yet deeper purple green and black green. Layer upon layer of color. For a moment I recall my mother's palette, her buildup of paint so that light could shine through. I see that light here in this place. Green folding in upon green.

Below the dreamy, lily-padded water lives a large snapping turtle. I have seen it cruising the bottom like a darkness within a darkness. It is somehow satisfying to think of its beak, its clawed feet moving indolently forward, the eyes and carapace almost unchanged in its species for millennia. I am afraid of and yet savor this wildness. The time of ancient beasts is still here in this suburban backyard. Dragonfly and snapping turtle. I feel stirred when I sense these connections and I feel hopeful too. Perhaps I haven't been tamed yet either.

I have time for reverie here, for gazing on the

world in a new way. I dream into the pond as into an eye. Minutes expand into hours, into time that is not measured. The dark water opens as if something were gazing back at me. I feel I am looking into the ground's eye, the eye of a huge presence. I am suddenly shy and very small. Exposed, stripped, not of my clothes, but of something else—of a layer that separates me from the world. I shiver and grow quiet. I feel naked and penetratingly seen.

To gaze into the eye of the ground itself, is it possible? Can the ground be aware of me? This is too strange to speak about. But I do sense the mutuality. This presence upholds my creatureliness . . . it knows that I breathe and move . . . that I cry and love . . . that I am afraid and exultant . . . that I create and destroy . . . that I hurt and take care. It knows! But not in any way that I can explain.

I feel an urgency now. I am compelled to notice everything. The wellspring that feeds the pond, and the land that holds this water. I am drawn into the sedge grass, the stones, the moss, and the tree roots that describe the edge of this place. I absorb the brown leaves that make the water dark and reflective. I am imprinted with the maple's shadow, plopped by frogs, sheltered by sky, and delighted by dragonflies. I am taken to the depth that mirrors my face back to me. And I sense the "snapper" moving like a mysterious cloud in the water.

This is happening inside me. The living water rises in my blood, the dragonfly whirs in my inner ear, the high-pitched joy of the peeper trills in my cells, the leaves mat and settle in my belly. I can feel how my life is a shared event. I am separate from nothing, not even the dead. Pondlike, reflective, who is this me? I don't know. I don't know. . . .

Noon. The heat seems to glaze the surface of the water. In the quiet and dark heart of the pond, Saint Snapper settles down. I wonder if deep inside me I am settling, too, learning to be fluid and yet still?

Day Lilies

*H*eight of summer. The day lilies are budding. They will soon come out. There are three varieties that will stagger their blooming from now until the beginning of August. All three are yellow: bright yellow. Butter yellow. And salmon yellow. They are a celebration of the sun at its zenith, their brief life an acknowledgment that each day is a unique blossom.

There is a ring of them near the crescent bed of peonies. There is a bank of them along one stone wall. And since they are profuse and readily multiply I have moved some to the bare place near the brook. I could have day lilies everywhere there is sun, just as I have impatiens everywhere there is shade.

Their stalks are thick and woody. Each one has several buds . . . the size of ladyfingers. One can eat these flowers. They have a mild, delicious flavor, as if one were tasting the sun. Their tubers can be dug up, and the small rhizomes they produce are also edible. They are nutty and white when young . . . like new potatoes.

Middle of summer is yellow-glory time. These lilies are bountiful. When I bring one in and put it in a vase, it illuminates my table, as though the sun were shining inside my house. Saint Glow. The lily will stay large and open until midnight. By morning, however, it is limp and wizened, and leaves a clear, round drop of moisture on the table. My finger touches it and I remember touching the corpse of my mother—the mystery of life passed on. I do not take these flowers for granted. It is all here together—my mother, this lily, and this day.

The solstice has passed. Now the year turns again toward the dark. More than ever I treasure these days as they grow shorter. In my own life I know I have fewer days left now than I have lived.

I look inside the yellowest of the lilies. It is trumpet-shaped. Looking deep I see the stamen, the pistil, and I see the mysterious darkness in the neck of the trumpet. Is it from there that all this yellow light pours out?

Black Snake

He lives in the stone wall. A very large snake. In the heat of late July he can sometimes be found baking on the stones. He has a drugged, sleepy quality when I find him in this state. He is letting his cold-blooded nature absorb the delicious warmth of these high summer days.

Black snake and I are friends. He does not bother me and I do not bother him, but we are aware of each other. He no longer slithers away when I find him. In this mutual living arrangement we admire each other, and keep the appropriate distance.

Other snakes have always frightened me, but this one does not. He seems a guardian. Every house should have its own black snake. I know he keeps the mice and chipmunk population down. But he does more. To me he is a representative of ancient wisdom. His very being reminds me that renewal is possible, that skins can and ought to be shed. I once found one of his . . . transparent . . . paper thin.

Black snake is elegant, whether coiled or moving. Like a small dark river he pours himself into the stone wall when he wants to, and is gone. The movement is sensuous. He flows himself forward, his belly feels and knows every inch of the ground. This is intimate indeed.

Sometimes I lie down on the grass to feel the ground with my own belly—in a kind of serpent connection. Skin on skin: earth skin, human skin.

To be held by earth, to shed your old skins and wait for the sun, to be cold when it is cold, to move quickly when it is time to move, and to lie about in happy indolence, this is black snake knowledge.

We meet at the stone wall . . . the warm-blooded one and the cold-blooded one . . . our domains joined for a moment. What do we have in common? The stones and the sun's warmth. The July air and the high cumulus clouds. We have this moment to be friends, to please each other. Black snake, I want you to know you please me very greatly.

Yellow Jackets

T here is now no picnic without at least three yellow jackets. It is the high heat of summer, the end of July. These insects hover around the food. They land in the fruit salad. They wedge themselves between the hamburger buns. Seemingly they will not be stopped.

These wasps have their nests in the ground. I have seen them fly into a very small hole in the bank under the wild roses. There is another nest under the pear tree. There may even be a third. Their nests are true "safe houses," and are strategically placed. The wasps can absorb their food and fly straight home.

It is curious to me that these insects like sugar

and meat in equal measure. Whatever they can take, they take. They are pesky pests. Saint Sting! I do not like the yellow jacket. I struggle with its species. I have poured gasoline into their homes and struck a match. My son, in an effort to help with this problem, was stung very terribly. Saint Yellow Jacket, I am stuck with your kind and I do not like you.

These wasps share my yard, my food, and my leisure . . . turning pleasant repasts into mobilizations for self-defense. Saint Sting affords me the opportunity to practice endurance and persistence.

Of course, I could forgo eating outside. But that gives these winged terrors too much power. And besides it is now very hot inside. What is it then that I endure? I do not believe it is Saint Sting actually. I have to endure my own discomfort and my fear of being stung, which fear is not unrealistic.

I have to endure interference with my personal rhythm. When I raise my fork to my mouth and a wasp goes with the eating utensil, I have to put it down. I have to wait. My eating pattern, and other patterns as well, are rattled.

I have to endure my guests' discomfort also. I find myself embarrassed that I have *wasps,* as if they were some communicable disease.

I have to endure the creepy feeling that my air space is being violated. One has a kinesthetic sense of how much space around the body is one's own . . . not unlike the air space and water rights of cities. These wasps are in my aura and I cannot keep them out.

In all this I can watch their persistence. They are not daunted by rolled newspapers, fly swatters, lemon-scented candles intended to discourage little flying things. They know where they are going. FOR THE STUFF!!!!!!!!!!!!!

If I could ever apply myself with similar concentration I would frighten myself. They have a kind of white heat about them. Their intensity matches the thermometer reading. Ninety degrees Fahrenheit and climbing. One hundred degrees of heat and concentration. I must take my sun hat off to these creatures of God's making. I acknowledge their right to be in this world, but I do not have to like them. Go away. Sting!

Vines

---

*H*oneysuckle and wild grape grow here in profusion. In and of themselves they are wonderful vines. The night air fills with honeysuckle sweetness, and by day bees visit them from my neighbor's hive. In August the grapes produce heavy purple clusters for jelly and the large, edible leaves for dolmades.

And yet the trees and bushes are choked by these vines. I am constantly having to cut them back. Whack! Whack! There is a persistent clinging going on here, to the point where some trees and bushes perish under the weight. I can feel how silently the vines take over if I am not on my guard.

When I go to prune them back I see how skillfully they wrap themselves clockwise around whatever is available. They are the opportunists of the garden, the hangers-on. Tendrils reach out to secure more growing territory. Up the trunk, over the branch, out into the air, searching for any cling-on place. No respecters of boundaries, these. They are the great enmeshers, thoughtless, relentless, helical, and wondrous.

I have to whack, and I do it with abandon. No nice careful pruning here. This is a machete kind of boundary setting that needs to be done on a regular basis. The pile of cut vines can grow to bonfire size. No reason to feel any compunction. They will be back. Whack!

I am struck by how hard it is for me to be similarly relentless when it comes to clinging people. There are always one or two with whom I struggle over boundaries. They are the honeysuckle and the grape in my personal relationships. I want them to be part of my life but I do not want them to weigh me to the ground.

I say no, politely, to begin with. I set up barriers. I raise my voice. Often the boundary is not respected, even then. So I go out into my garden to study the vines. I see and verify that the nature of honeysuckle and grape is to climb, to grow *upon* something. They cannot be other than how they are. Therefore they must be contained in a proper way. I do not need to get angry about this. I just have to do the job. But I am not a whacker by nature. So this is hard.

When I think about it, we are all actually vine-like. We grow upon the strength of others, reaching out for new places of discovery. Our need for support is constant. I want to remember that there is no skipping the boundary setting, even with nearest and dearest. This is "tough love" for me.

But when I study the vines in my garden I see that they actually become stronger the more I contain them. Rather than spreading farther out, the vines gain substance. They get thicker and sturdier. They hold themselves up a little better. I want to trust what I see. I want to trust that this also happens when I refuse to let people take advantage of me, disregard me, or assume that I am continually available for support.

Whack! I shiver at the pruning task. It is so deliberate, so steely, so necessary. I hurt for myself and for the other. Whack! The feeling of being weighed down goes. Whack! Enmeshments go. Whack! Hard as it is, we grow stronger for the pruning.

And the summer nights continue warm and full of stars. I smell the honeysuckle through my window. I am glad. And in the morning I go hunting for the young grapes. They are filling out, plump and dusty purple.

Cicadas

Now in the cycle of seasons since my mother's death the anniversary of her birthday comes. August fifth. I light a candle for her and feel bereft. I miss her greatly, miss her laugh, her big warm hands, her lust for life. I miss her shape in a doorway. I miss the way she walked, tiptoeing lightly like a girl, even in her portly seventies. To know she is no longer is strange. It makes the world itself strange.

The heat has been relentless. Everything seems to pant or wilt or move with appalling effort. At night the cicadas have started their chorus. It is a rather quiet chorus to begin with, but as summer progresses toward autumn the singing seems to intensify, till nights are filled to capacity by the chorus. Each night is a chamber of sound—waves move into each other and also echo one another. Sound arises and falls away, only to return again. How many cicadas are out there? How many?

I feel sad now. Burdened, actually. The heat has something to do with it. I do not want to move my body and yet I must bear up. It's too hot to work, to play, to plant, to do anything at all. I feel as if I am both in the bed and by the bed of someone dying. A truly helpless feeling.

August is often when wars start, when old folks die, when there are violent storms. Everything seems to have difficulty enduring itself. Ripeness is a burdensome state. It has too much potential violence in it.

Many people go away on vacation now. I feel I cannot do anything about anything. I might as well lie in the hammock and listen to cicadas singing out their monotony, their exultation. This is their time . . . the chanting time.

I think of ceremonies I have attended where the drum held a beat for hours, and the same song was sung until one gave into it, until the inner door swung wide and another dimension opened up. Scientific theories tell how a critical mass must be arrived at before a new paradigm can be discovered. If this is true for science, for creativity, and for consciousness, it must be true for the state of grief also. I live each day and feel the hum of life around me, and I feel my mother's absence just as keenly.

One bears grief in whatever way one can, as long as one must. Silently it accumulates. If it has no direct means of expression it will come out in an illness, in an accident, in the rupture of a relationship. Grief ripens like a fruit. It must be harvested in some way. We need company to do this, for to grieve alone only drives the pain into a deeper place.

The cicadas are wailing. This is my time to feel the weight of grief. This season I need a friend to be with, someone who will not be shocked if I keen too. I want to wail in waves like the cicadas, and let the grief out so I can hear it . . . the grief of such loss, the grief of all that suffers . . . the salutary grief that when acknowledged gives relief, an opening to life.

Honeybells

*A*long the stone wall grow the hosta. They have been filling out more and more as the years go by. Big leaves emerge in May and get larger, until by June a deep bank of green lines the wall. Some of the leaves have dark edges, some are as big as elephant ears.

These plants give shape to the garden. They are large, handsome, and sturdy. Their flowers smell sweet. On moonlit nights, late like this in the summer, you can see the whitish purple bells shine back. They deserve the name the nursery gave them, honeybell.

When they have gone by, the flowers produce

seeds that birds like. All in all these are steady, no-fuss, no-work plants that make the garden look shapely and complete no matter what may or may not be blooming.

As a consequence these hosta are easy to take for granted. Anything strong, steady, reliable, constant, is taken for granted. There is an of-course-you'll-continue-to-be-there attitude one develops with such dependability.

There are people who are like these plants. We do not even know how much we count on them. They are the background, the backbone, the backup. And they become somehow invisible to us in their strength and willingness to serve. We are totally surprised if anything happens to them. We are shocked, in fact.

One year some deer came in July and munched up the hosta. The leaves had come to maturity, and since all the succulent greens had been exhausted in the woods, the deer came to help themselves to this ready green grocery. I woke up that morning and found what looked like trimmed celery stalks. No large green elephant leaves. No dense green sculpture. Only stalks! The place was devastated.

After that I took more care. I got human hair from the barber to put on the ground. (The smell is said to discourage the deer.) I began to appreciate the stately shapes of these sturdy plants. I began to care more for them than for the annuals. I no longer took their steady presence for granted.

And I have to think now about relationships I have taken for granted. My mother certainly. Old friends. People in the helping professions whom I expect to be reliable: my dentist, my doctor, the person who does my taxes, the man who has cut the grass for years. They form the background to my foreground, and I understand how much I have not realized the shape that they give my life.

Saint Honeybell. The stems of hosta flowers are waving in the August breeze. A sweet aroma wafts over my garden wall. This delicate odor is the silent ringing of these bells. "Wake up," they say. "Hear the bell. Appreciate us. There is yet time."

Harvest

Cucumbers, tomatoes, basil, eggplant, peppers, beets, New Zealand spinach. The crops are coming in now. I have not done so well with the vegetable garden, but well enough to feel rushed, to want to use the produce, to invite people over to help me eat it.

The nasturtiums are in full bloom. Their snappy leaves and flowers fill the salad bowl. The tomatoes are bulging with juice. The pears are yellowing. The plums have already gone by. There is plenty now. It's bounty time. When the time for bounty is here I must not dread what might come next. This is the time to open wide, to harvest, to share, to be as flagrant as nature. It is early September, the time of ripeness when all hangs ready on the plant. Take it.

As I pick cucumbers, their prickly skins caress my hand. My eggplants hang in purple splendor, not as big this year as other times, but glossy and silky of skin. I remember when they were only mauve four-petaled flowers. I pop a nasturtium in my mouth. "Nasty urchins," as my friend Joyce calls them. The roof of my mouth pings with the stimulation. My basket is full of saints. Each mature vegetable or fruit has touched me first as seedling or seed. As they grew, I grew. We have ripened together.

I gather this harvest to me. I will consume it and make it part of my very flesh even as I harvest experience and it, too, becomes part of my very being. I know I live by consuming life. And life is living me, consuming me.

I hold the bounty basket in my arms. On top are the nasturtium flowers. They move in the breeze that has just come over the hill. The red, yellow, orange flowers roll to the basket's rim. Quickly I put a hand over them so they will not blow to the ground. The breeze picks up. The petals shiver. My basket is full. It is all so precious and impermanent. With my hand over this riot of color, I feel this year—the grief and the joy of it—the great bounty.

FALL AGAIN

Compost

Now I weed out the flower beds, getting ready for the frost. The vegetable garden has been turned over. The impatiens are setting seed pods. In my fist these pods explode like small, green firecrackers. Freed, the little black seeds lie in the crevice of my hand, highlighting the crease the palmists call the lifeline.

Small songbirds help themselves to the honeybell seeds, and squirrels are avidly gathering acorns. I pop the last of the late raspberries into my mouth. They are poignantly sweet. Now the ash tree boletus emerge from the ground, and puffballs. These mushrooms are edible, and I harvest them, too.

It's cleanup time. I trudge with my wheelbarrow up to the compost pile—a handsome heap by now. Leaves have begun to fall. I bring vegetable scraps and garden remains to this, my kitchen midden. The leaves from last year are now flattened on the ground, somewhat decomposed, and underneath all is a haven for earthworms. I turn the compost with the pitchfork. I see the black earth and the slow undulating movement of the worms. They are long and fat at this time of year. Science tells us that by mass there are more worms than any other living thing.

I lift the top layer of leaves with the pitchfork. The work of decomposition has been going on quietly all these months—a silent heat. It has broken down all the old organic material and there is new earth here. I will put this soil on the garden come spring. But now I bring my prunings, gleanings, and kitchen scraps, and pile them up. Soon leaves will cover everything and the slow transformation will continue, the composting of another year.

Twelve months have passed. I have lived all the seasons. Standing here in this kitchen midden, knee-high in leaves, I know this year now joins all the other years. It's fall again. The geese fly over, heading south. Their honking lifts my spirits. I think of my mother and somehow I feel her presence inside me. I know now that everything that was is still present in some fundamental and mysterious way.

This is intimacy: its touch is ever new, revealing the precious moments we have to live and to connect with all things. No love is ever lost in this universe. No matter what season, what year, what place, love will always be turned into new soil. Grateful to the saints of this place, and feeling intimacy grow with all that lives and has lived here, I hold my mother closely in my heart and mind, and I sense the passion, the silent becoming in this compost, in the living of the years.

GUNILLA NORRIS is a psychotherapist in private practice. Besides the books in this volume, she is the author of *Being Home: A Book of Meditations,* eleven children's books, and a book of poems, *Learning from the Angel.* She lives in Mystic, Connecticut.